STANDING FOR YOUR MARRIAGE

When You Say I DO

God Says I WILL

God's Covenant Gives Power to Say "I Won't" to Divorce

by
Bob Christensen
and Ron Griego, Sr.

ISBN 1-8860-4514-3
Printed in the United States of America

Scripture quotations are from the *King James Version* of the Bible unless otherwise noted.

For information, write:
Covenant Marriages Ministry
17301 W. Colfax, Suite 140
Golden, CO 80401

Names and certain facts used in anecdotal illustrations in this manuscript have been altered to protect the privacy of those involved.

To

Dedicated to all the men and women who have uncompromisingly chosen to believe and stand for the will and purposes of God in their marriage, and in the marriages of others.

We wish particularly to honor those Pastors who have chosen to raise God's banner higher by going against the popular attitude that breaking covenant is an acceptable alternative to upholding God's plan for marriage.

We especially honor our wives, Lynn Christensen and Dora Griego, whom we love with all our hearts and with whom we walk in covenant.

CONTENTS

Endorsement For
"When You Say I Do, God Says I Will"

What a joy to know that God is still in the "healing business". He not only heals sick bodies but He heals sick marriages as well.

As you read Bob's new book, you will be inspired and encouraged to stand on God's Word to strengthen your marriage and make it what He always intended it to be.

Thanks Bob, for showing us that marriage can and should be the greatest experience that a man and a woman could ever hope to have.

Jerry Savelle

Some parts read like a romantic love novel, others like a theological perspective on covenant agreements and relationships. This is a book that can speak to both men and women.

When You Say I Do, God Says I Will allows us to understand marriage, its joys, and responsibilities from a new perspective. The most profound message is that a marriage takes three to be successful. We can't do it without giving the full burden to the Lord Jesus Christ.

"Dr. Bob" is one of the most phenomenal men I've ever met - brilliant surgeon, perky television personality, and now vibrant author. He and co-author Ron Griego Sr. just sparkle with the love of the Lord. Their energy, enthusiasm, and sincerity are contagious and should be trusted as they lead us into new ways of looking at the marriage covenant. Their own experiences, so richly retold, are living examples of this biblical truth.

Julie Baker
Executive Producer,
Time Out - For Women Only

This new book on the Marriage Covenant is well overdue. With the collapsing of marriages and relationships across the entire world, it comes as a breath of fresh air that someone is taking the matter seriously. To suggest as some do that the only people affected in divorce are the two parties involved is grossly misleading as the children, friends, relatives and even business associates all seem to be entangled in some way by making conversation, invitations and even at times, preferences for and against the divorced or the divorcing partner. Our law courts are overburdened with divorce settlements and attorneys are waiting like vultures to bicker over the spoils while in the process gaining their own rewards.

In business, contracts are broken with great penalty and a cost to all concerned, and yet the penalties and costs of a broken marriage can go on for a lifetime, but are never reconciled. The commitments of a man and a woman by way of a marriage covenant for life has God's signature upon it and was one of the earliest acts of creation, so that mankind could live, populate and subdue the earth in harmony and security. The act of a covenant marriage with its love, responsibility and stability is also the cement that holds a nation together. Without stability, trust and affection on the home front, the process filters through to the governments as they become shaky, as distrust and insecurity extends throughout all areas of life.

What this book has to offer is a deeper, more meaningful and studied look at the principles of marriage in a society that tends to accept and even "trend set" the divorce procedure while ignoring the biblical specifics which God created in His Heavenly wisdom for our benefit.

As Christians we are losing the battle for the propagation of our faith, not because of lack of church attendance or being able to quote scripture or even in what we say or sing, but because we have lost the concept of love in a committed relationship called a covenant marriage for life.

Read and re-read this book, and open your mind and heart to the seriousness of such a covenant. I thoroughly endorse and recommend this book.

Peter J Daniels
Founder and President
World Centre for Entrepreneurial Studies
International Business Statesman
14 April 1998

Introduction

Introduction

Say "Yes" to a Covenant Marriage!

This is a book that advocates marriage.

If you are contemplating marriage, it is a book that will build your understanding and faith to believe God for a covenant marriage that will last all your life.

If you are married and are experiencing difficulties in your marriage, it is a book that will build your understanding and faith to believe that God will fulfill the promises related to the covenant of marriage that you have entered.

If you are separated, or even divorced, it is a book that will help you continue to believe God for a full reconciliation of your heart to that of your spouse, and whenever possible, a full restoration of your marriage.

God desires to see His Kingdom established first and foremost in our families – in our marriages and in the relationship between parents and children. That is the primary proving ground of God's Word. It is the first place where one's faith is to be applied and strengthened. As the family is strong in Christ, so the church to which that family belongs will become stronger in Christ. As the church becomes strong, so the community in which the church is located will become stronger. The family, however, is at the core of God's Kingdom-building efforts.

The Binding
Force of Covenant

One of the most important binding forces of marriage, and in turn, a very potent "glue" that holds a family together, is covenant.

Most people with whom we have had contact in the last twenty years do not understand the meaning of a marriage covenant. They say they believe in marriage. They even admit to having made marriage vows, and will state that they believe in their vows, but they do not understand the deep spiritual meaning of covenant relationship – either with God, or with a spouse.

Covenant is a spiritual concept, initiated by God. It is God's "method" for bringing a man and woman into lasting relationship with Himself, and with each other.

Covenant is also a living reality. Not only is covenant initiated by God, it is "executed" by God. In other words, God enables covenant to become a present reality in our lives. He indwells the covenant relationship with His own presence, purposes, power, and will. God makes covenant happen.

Once God establishes covenant with a person or group of people, He never abandons the covenant relationship. All of the provisions and promises associated with covenant are ours forever.

The Uniqueness in
Christian Marriage

A marriage covenant between two persons bears strong similarities to an individual's spiritual covenant with God. This is especially true for Christians. Why? Because when two Christians enter into a covenant of marriage with each other, God becomes a part of that covenant. Indeed, He is the One who extends to the covenant of marriage the same types of provisions and promises that He has already extended to each person. He is the One who truly unites the two so that they become one flesh in His eyes. He is the One who brings to bear all of the power and provisions of covenant on their relationship.

Two Christians who are married to each other cannot leave God outside their marriage. God will always be the unseen, silent, supportive, always loving, and generous Lord of the marriage.

Therefore, this is not only a book that advocates and supports marriage, but it is aimed specifically at Christians who are married or who are contemplating marriage.

In many ways, a Christian has a different status of marriage than a non-Christian just as a Christian lives a different life than a non-Christian. Jesus Christ not only enables a covenant to be forged between a husband and wife, but He enables that covenant relationship to be fulfilled through the power of the Holy Spirit residing in the lives of the husband and wife.

While there are no doubt many good teachings in this book that can help people who are not Christians, or which apply to marriages in which one person is a Christian and the other is not, the message in this book is primarily for Christians.

Before you conclude that Christians do not need a book about the sanctity of the marriage covenant because they already believe in the covenant and do not divorce, consider the statistics related to marriages today! Nearly a third of all adults in the United States are currently divorced or were divorced prior to their current marriage. Nearly one-half of all those who are married say that they have had times of serious disagreement or difficulties in their marriages which have led them to contemplate separation or divorce, even if they have not acted on that idea. These statistics related to marriage in general are not all that different from the statistics for those married people who attend church — in fact, they differ by only a few percentage points.

The conclusion must be drawn that many people who are in the church or who call themselves Christians do not have happy marriages. Christians are separating and divorcing at far too high a rate. Even pastors and those in church leadership are falling victim to the "divorce avalanche."

Surely no one would agree that divorce is God's will, especially when God states so plainly throughout His Word that the hardness of heart and sin that lead to divorce are contrary to His highest plan for men and women. Yet as a whole, we in the church have readily accepted divorce as a means to resolving human conflict.

"Divorce recovery" programs are very popular within Christian churches today. Rather than pursue divorce recovery, why not pursue marriage recovery? Why not believe God to restore the marriage, rather than heal the divorce? Why not stand for a full reconciliation within the covenant promises of God, rather than seek a way to negate or set aside covenant vows?

We are in a losing position today regarding marriage. Many within the church as a whole have taken the position that divorce is not only a reality, but also even desirable in some cases. We have lost sight of the power of covenant, and furthermore, the power available through the keeping of covenant.

We need to state with great boldness regarding our marriages –

No judge, attorney, nor the devil has the authority, ability, or power to destroy a marriage covenant blessed by God and upheld by the love and confession of a faithful husband or wife no matter how eloquently the word divorce may be pronounced.

So many Christians accept the dissolution of their marriage covenant as a "fact" when a judge declares in a secular court that they are divorced. These same Christians, however, would never dream of believing a judge who would tell them that their covenant relationship with the Heavenly Father was broken, dissolved, or beyond reconciliation . . . regardless of reason.

We need to see our Christ-centered marriages as being just as binding as our relationship with Christ, for indeed, Christ is a part of a marriage that is rooted in Him. A marriage between two Christians does not involve those two people alone – it is a "threefold cord" that includes the binding power of God Himself. Just as the Lord has bound Himself to each person in the marriage, so He unites the two as one in Him.

This book advocates that we say "yes" – with loud and resounding voices – to covenant marriage. For it is our contention that if we ever truly grasp the meaning of covenant, and especially as it applies to marriage, we will see a great change not only in our marriage relationships, but in our families, our communities, our churches, and our nation!

Chapter 1

CHAPTER 1

Recognizing God's Role in Your Marriage

One of the greatest lessons that any person can ever learn is that he or she cannot do anything alone or in one's own strength. It simply is not possible. Another person is always involved – as a motivator for action, a partner in action, an onlooker to action, or an object of action. Furthermore, God is always a required partner in bringing about anything that has a benefit or that might be considered good.

This is especially important for you to recognize when it comes to your marriage covenant. You cannot fulfill your marriage covenant on your own. Not only is your spouse involved, but God is also involved in the covenant agreement. You are part of a threefold entity. By yourself, you cannot make your marriage "good." To make anything good requires the presence and work of God.

Very specifically, you cannot keep problems from arising in your marriage . . . by yourself. You cannot resolve problems in a healthful, beneficial, good manner . . . by yourself. You cannot keep problems from reoccurring . . . by yourself. God must be included in the process. Indeed, it is God who will do the definitive work of perfecting you, even as He does the definitive work of perfecting your marriage.

Furthermore, if your marriage has fallen apart to the point where you are separated from your spouse, or even divorced legally, you cannot by yourself bring about a restoration of your marriage. God must not only be invited to participate actively in the process of restoring your marriage, but your total reliance must be upon Him. Only God can truly change a human heart – both yours and that of your spouse. Only God can bring about a change in desire, a refocusing of priorities, and renewed love.

Any good thing that you are able to do either to build up and reinforce your existing marriage, or to attempt a restoration of your marriage, will occur only as you allow God to work in you and through you. He is the potter; you are the clay. He is the master designer; you are the work of His hands. He is the One who gives life. He is the author and finisher of the good work He has begun in you.

By yourself, you are highly limited in power. With God, you are in covenant with One who has unlimited power. He can do what you cannot do.

Many years ago, both of us – Bob and Ron – came to this understanding that God was our source and foundation of a good marriage. We have come to our understanding of covenant marriage not only from years of Bible study, but also from personal experience.

In sharing our stories with you, we trust you will not only have a new awareness of how God's presence and power can transform a marriage, but that you will have renewed or greater hope for your own marriage relationship.

Ron's Story – A Total Healing

Dora and I fell in love when we were teenagers and we married after only three months of courtship when we were only nineteen and eighteen years old. In many ways we were like two unknowns colliding, but we knew one thing: we were in love.

Within a few years, we had two children and our lives took on a distinct pattern.

I pursued a military career and enjoyed a great deal of success in the military. I received several promotions and won a number of awards and commendations, and I fully expected to be a "career man" in the armed forces. To virtually everybody who may have watched my life from afar, I seemed to be a "good" man who was doing just fine in his life. I thought of myself that way! What others could not see were my vices, which at the time I considered to be quite minor: drinking, marijuana, and partying. Although I promised Dora repeatedly that I would give up alcohol, drugs, and my partying friends, I had no inner strength to turn my promises into reality.

Religion played little part in our married life although Dora felt that a faith in God was very important since she had been taught that during her childhood. She also had spent years wondering if there was "more" to life than the loneliness she felt in her heart.

Then, our lives began to unravel.

Dora fell and ruptured discs in her back when she was in her early thirties. Her hospitalization was prolonged and the prognosis was that she likely would be confined to a wheelchair for the rest of her life. Our children were sent to my parents in a neighboring city since I could not care for the children and work full-time. My drinking now became an escape, not just a pleasurable pastime, and alcohol soon became a problem for me – the drinking was becoming the focal point of my life although it gave me little satisfaction.

Things came to a head the weekend that Dora's physicians suggested that I take her home for the weekend. They could see that Dora was becoming depressed at her long stay in the hospital and although they were not ready to release her completely, they felt a weekend visit at home would lift her spirits.

No sooner had I brought Dora home, however, that I left her to go out drinking with my friends. When I returned home in the wee hours of the following morning, I found my wife emotionally crushed. She asked me why I had even bothered to bring her home.

I knew that Dora's search for God had increased in fervency during her hospitalization. She felt very depressed at the thought of being confined to a wheelchair the rest of her life, and being with a drinking and partying husband. A friend gave her a copy of the famous poem, "Footprints in the Sand," and it touched Dora's heart. She knew she needed someone to "carry" her through the struggle in which she found herself.

Out of guilt for my bad behavior the previous day, I offered to take Dora to a little storefront church that my brother had told me about. I was hoping to make amends.

My brother had been my drinking buddy until he gave his life to Jesus Christ, at which point he gave up alcohol and frequently witnessed to me about the love of Jesus. Although I could see a tremendous change in his life, I rejected the Gospel he shared so eagerly with me. I truly felt I was fine just the way I was and that I did not need religion as a "crutch."

When Dora and I entered that little church in June 1981, I had no idea what might be waiting for us. The preacher was a wild-eyed little man who paced the floor as he spoke. He first announced that he was going to preach, and then he abruptly changed course and told us he had decided to teach. No sooner had he started to teach than he changed course again and told us he was going to tell his life story and what God had done for him. I had such a headache from being hung over, and I just wished he'd do something so we could get out of there sooner rather than later!

As the preacher began to tell his story, I felt as if he were telling my story. He seemed to have felt and experienced much of what I had been through, with one difference – he had invited God to be in his life. And what a difference that had seemed to make!

When the time came for the service to end, the preacher invited those present to commit their lives to the Lord and to accept Jesus Christ as their Savior. Well, apart from this man's wife and daughter, Dora and I were the only people in the room! Dora quickly moved to make this commitment. She had been seeking God for some time and this opportunity was exactly what she had desired. For my part, I could hardly wait to get out the front door. Even so, I found myself responding to the preacher's invitation before the service ended – mostly to "get it over with," not out of conviction.

To my great surprise, when I responded to the altar call and the preacher began to pray for us with great spiritual fervor and power, I began to weep. I'm not at all the crying type, but that night I couldn't hold back the tears. The preacher prayed to God as if He knew God personally. It was unlike any prayer that either Dora or I had ever heard before. As I cried, I thought, "God, I want You to be as real to me as You are to this preacher." I opened my heart to God.

After having prayed for Dora and me to accept Christ, the preacher noticed the hospital wristband on Dora's arm and he asked if he could pray for Dora's healing. Dora didn't feel anything at the time the preacher prayed for her, but that night as she lay in her makeshift bed in the living room of our apartment, she prayed, "God, I need Your help." Even as she was praying downstairs, I was crying and praying upstairs, "God, I need for my wife to be healed." I felt completely drained of energy and emotions at that point. I truly had reached the end of myself and with a genuine and sincere heart, I was reaching out to God.

After Dora prayed, she got out of bed and began to move around, and as she moved, she noticed immediately that she had no pain. No matter which way she moved her body, she felt no pain! She climbed the stairs to our second-floor bedroom, which she had been unable to do before. She said to me, "I think I've been healed!" We could hardly believe it! God had given us the two miracles we needed – salvation for our souls, and healing for Dora's body.

In the days that followed, I discarded all of the alcohol, cigars, and marijuana-related items I had in our apartment. Nobody told me to do this – I just knew in my spirit that it was the right thing to do.

When I took Dora back to the hospital, people from throughout the ward came to see her. Needless to say, they were all surprised to see her walking freely, with a big smile on her face as she announced, "I've been healed." The doctor arrived as Dora was packing the things in her hospital room and asked, "What's going on?" Dora replied simply, "Jesus healed me."

The physician had her move in various ways and although he told me that I was a fool for believing that God had healed Dora, he did agree to sign her release papers from the hospital. He also predicted that she would return within two weeks. That was seventeen years ago and Dora has never been back to the hospital!

Although we have experienced life's problems and challenges just as any other couple, we both have felt from that point onward a strong reliance upon Jesus Christ to build up and strengthen our marriage and our family relationships. We began to attend church and Bible studies, and as a couple, we also read the Bible together.

In the months following our salvation and Dora's healing, I felt the Lord calling me to preach. I gave up my military career and we moved to Texas to pioneer a church. We were also in an evangelistic ministry for a period, and then, we met Bob Christensen. As Bob and I began to study the Scriptures about marriage and covenant relationships, we both realized anew the importance of this message. The covenant is what has kept my marriage with Dora strong as the years have gone by. Bob had this same understanding about covenant and marriage.

As far as I am concerned there is no more valuable teaching for marriages today than a teaching about God's covenant relationship with His people.

Bob's Story – A Need for More of God and His Word

I learned about the power of God's covenant much the same way Ron and Dora did, and most people do – out of tragedy and conflict.

My life as an oral surgeon seemed to be a good one. I had a thriving practice in northern California. I flew my own pressurized Cessna P-210 airplane for fun. I felt I "had it all together."

Then in 1983, my mother died while I was laid up in a hospital bed. During that same time, my wife left me and took our children with her. I was devastated. Suddenly, I felt lost. Nothing made sense in my life.

Wanting to be near my family, I left my practice and moved to southern California where my wife had gone. My finances were collapsing around me and I was on the verge of losing everything, either through divorce or bankruptcy.

In the light of all that was happening to me, I did what

appeared to be a very stupid thing – I went to a flight school to learn how to fly jets. It was the turning point of my life.

My instructor's name was Dale Black. More important than his knowledge of jets was the fact that Dale knew the Lord. His example, and his words to me, during that one week of flight instruction brought me to the point of praying for Christ to come into my life.

Dale had recently seen God work a miracle in restoring his own broken marriage. Before I left the flight school, he gave me a Bible with the names of both my wife and me imprinted on the cover. On the inside of the Bible, Dale inscribed, "Presented to Robert and Lynne Christensen by Dale and Paula Black on October 25, 1983, in faith, believing for your family's unity." That was the starting point of my believing for my own family's unity!

As I drove home from the flight school the night Dale gave me this Bible, I saw a license plate that said, "UZMEGOD." (Use me, God.) I immediately made that my prayer.

I had planned to see Lynne regarding our financial settlement the next day. We had a number of issues to discuss regarding the divorce she was seeking, but more than feeling a concern about the negotiation that lay ahead, I felt an excitement at the thought of seeing her. As I drove to the restaurant where we had agreed to meet, I saw another license plate that triggered my faith. It said, "GODFRST." (God first.) I made that my priority for our meeting.

I shared with Lynne the changes that were taking place in my life and I sensed a spark of renewed hope in her that things between us might improve.

Day by day, God began to lead me in my new adventure of faith.

One of the pressing needs I had at that time was a need for transportation. I started to pray for a car, and very specifically, for a VW Rabbit. Shortly thereafter, a man I barely knew made it possible for me to have the very make and model I had requested from God, even though I didn't have either a job or money at the time. I made a sign and placed it on the back of the car: "Jesus Lives – He gave me this car."

My faith was growing, of course, for more than a car. I began to believe for a full restoration of all that I had lost in my life.

Soon, I had a job. Then I found a house that was only three blocks from Lynne and the children. Perhaps most miraculously of all, God began to renew a love in my heart for my wife.

At that time, we had been separated for two years. Bitterness had every opportunity to creep into my heart, and yet, God seemed to be doing an opposite work: He was breathing hope and love into our relationship.

One night I dreamed that Lynne was dying of thirst and in my dream, I was frantic in my search for water to save her. I shared this dream with Christian friends, and as I did, I realized that the water that truly would save Lynne was the water to which Jesus had referred when He spoke to the woman at the well in Sychar – Lynne was in need of the same "living water" of salvation that I had needed so desperately in my life. I began to see every encounter with Lynne as an opportunity to express God's love to her. The more I sought to share God's love with Lynne, the more love I felt for her in my own heart. It was a cycle that built and built, higher and higher, stronger and stronger.

Then on March 24, 1985 – two years after Lynne had left – the Lord spoke quietly but convincingly to Lynne's spirit. He said, "It's time to go home." She packed her belongings, the children, the cats, and the dog, and drove the three blocks to my doorstep.

When I opened the door, she said simply, "I have come home."

The next several years were a glorious odyssey. Four years after our marriage was restored, we moved to Colorado with little more than faith and a promise. We started a medical device company alongside a fledgling ministry, which we called Covenant Marriages Ministry.

Our little company soon outgrew the basement of our home into a facility of its own at the foot of the Rocky Mountains in Golden, Colorado. More important to us than the renewed flow of finances into our lives was the flow of the Holy Spirit into us. Doors opened repeatedly for us to minister to others whose marriages were in trouble. We eventually began a daily television program to carry the message of covenant marriage to Denver and other cities.

Through our years of ministry, two messages have continually filled our hearts:

- We each need more of God.
- We each need a greater understanding of God's Word.

We Need More of God

Every person alive – no matter how long he or she has been a Christian – needs more of God. Most people think they need more money, more happiness, or "more" of something else they believe they are lacking in order to feel better about themselves or to have a better marriage. What we really need is more of God – individually and as couples. There isn't a marriage today that can't benefit from each partner having a more intimate relationship with God.

The prophet Hosea gave these words of the Lord, "My people are destroyed for lack of knowledge" (Hosea 4:6). Our loss – of hope, of love, of finances, of security, of a marriage – always begins with a loss of understanding about who God is and what

He desires for us and from us.

The only way any person, including any Christian, can have a vital and fulfilling life is to have a flow of God's knowledge coming into his or her life on a daily basis.

The enemy of our souls is always going to be present to stalk us and roar against us. But when we have a working knowledge of God's presence – which means that we know His Word and we have a sure knowing in our spirits that God is with us – we are able to defeat the enemy at every turn.

During the days when Lynne and I were separated, I came to a vast new understanding of God's love for me, His love for Lynne, and of the truth that God is bigger than any problem that tries to destroy love. God has linked Himself to us, and He will neither leave us nor forsake us. Therefore, with His help we can overcome any circumstance we face, no matter how terrible it may be.

We Each Need Greater Understanding of God's Word

As Christians, our lives are to be anchored in God's Word. In the same way, our marriages must be anchored in the Word.

In the weeks and months after I prayed to receive Jesus as my Savior, I had a growing desire to read God's Word. I began also to cross paths with people who, like me, had faced broken relationships and had seen God heal them. One of these was Gavin MacLeod of "Love Boat" fame, who later was my best man when Lynne and I restated our wedding vows.

During our separation, I saw how powerful was the Word of God to each person I met who was standing in faith for their marriages to be reconciled, restored, or healed. Specific verses of Scripture were like "anchors" for their hope. In every case, they chose to believe God's Word more than they chose to believe the circumstances or situations around them.

Scriptures such as these became ones that I memorized and either spoke or thought many times in any given week:

Delight thyself also in the Lord and he shall give thee the desires of thine heart

Psalm 37:4

Weeping may endure for a night, but joy cometh in the morning

Psalm 30:5

[Jesus said], *"Have faith in God.*

For verily I say unto you, That whosoever shall say unto this mountain, Be thou removed, and be thou cast into the sea; and shall not doubt in his heart, but shall believe that those things which he saith shall come to pass; he shall have whatsoever he saith"

Mark 11:22-23

I took the Word of God seriously. I saw every verse as applying to me, and as being important to my life.

At the close of each chapter in this book you are going to find Scripture verses that we hope you will memorize and recall frequently to your mind and heart. Not only is it important to know God's truth about covenant, but it is vitally important to be able to use God's Word in believing for God's best related to your life and marriage.

The concepts related to covenant marriage are Bible concepts. They are not man's idea, but rather, God's idea. If we truly want to have good marriages, we must come to a clear understanding that

God is a full partner in our marriage relationships. He is in covenant with us. The more we recognize His role and receive His help, the more we will experience everything we might determine as being important or beneficial to our marriage.

God's purpose for man from the beginning of creation has been for man to have dominion over the earth and all other living creatures. The devil stole that dominion from Adam and Eve when they disobeyed God. The Bible characterizes the devil repeatedly as a thief and a murderer whose desire is to destroy us and keep us from entering into the fullness of all that God has for us. As a part of his plan, the devil seeks to keep men and women out of a covenant relationship with God, and therefore, strip them of the power that is related to a covenant relationship.

Keeping God's Word alive in your mind and in your speech is a way of reminding yourself that you are in a covenant relationship with God and that He, being your covenant partner in marriage is greater than any force that comes against you.

Scriptures That Confirm:

God Is Your Partner for a Good Marriage

A threefold cord is not quickly broken

Ecclesiastes 4:12

How precious is your constant love, O God! All humanity takes refuge in the shadow of your wings.

You feed them with blessings from your own table and let them drink from your rivers of delight.

For you are the Fountain of life; our light is from your Light.

Pour out your unfailing love on those who know you! Never stop giving your salvation to those who long to do your will

Psalm 36:7-10 (TLB)

I am the vine, ye are the branches: He that abideth in me, and I in him, the same bringeth forth much fruit: for without me ye can do nothing

John 15:5

Ye have not chosen me, but I have chosen you, and ordained you, that ye should go and bring forth fruit, and that your fruit should remain: that whatsoever ye shall ask of the Father in my name, he may give it you

John 15:16

But we have this treasure in earthen vessels, that the excellency of the power may be of God, and not of us.

We are troubled on every side, yet not distressed; we are perplexed, but not in despair;

persecuted, but not forsaken; cast down, but not destroyed;

always bearing about in the body the dying of the Lord Jesus, that the life also of Jesus might be made manifest in our body

2 Corinthians 4:7-10

Chapter 2

Chapter 2

God: The Covenant Maker

We must never lose sight of the fact that God, and God alone, initiated the covenant He has with mankind. If you are in relationship with God today, it is because God took the initiative to establish that relationship with you.

Many people ask, "What do I have to do to approach God?" All of the major religions of the world attempt to answer this question. The answers vary but at the core of every answer is a scheme, ritual, or "path" proclaiming: "Here is what you must do to approach God." Judaism and Christianity differ from all other religions in a very important way: They teach that God first approached man.

God came to Abraham and said, "I have chosen you." All of the movement toward a relationship came from God's side. Abraham's sole activity in establishing relationship with God was to believe. That was all he did, and it was counted as sufficient. In Galatians 3:6 we read, "Even as Abraham believed God, and it was accounted to him for righteousness." Abraham simply put his faith and trust in what God had done and was doing.

What God asks of us in establishing a covenant relationship is that we come into AGREEMENT with Him — that we agree to the description in the Bible of who He is, who we are, and what type of relationship we are to have with Him. In other words, God extends Himself to us and He asks only that we receive Him and align ourselves with Him.

Agreeing with God's Plan

God did not create the universe and all that is in it without a plan. Neither does He create any human being without having a plan for that person's life. God is purposeful. He has a design in mind.

The same is true for your marriage and all other relationships that exist in your life. God has a plan for you and for for every person with whom you are in relationship. He has a purpose for your being married to precisely the person you have married. That purpose is ultimately for your good. It is also for the good of the other person, and ultimately it is for the good of the children you may bear together or the spiritual children you may "birth" into the Kingdom of God.

God also has a plan for entering into a covenant relationship with you. He seeks to establish covenant with you so that you might become a vessel for expressions of His love, blessing, and power to other people.

God's call to each of us is that we discover and fulfill His purpose for our life, and that we come into a greater awareness of the reason for our marriage and the reason that God has entered into covenant with us.

What Is a Covenant?

Most people seem to think that a covenant is a contract. Those who own homes know that the neighborhoods in which they reside have certain "covenants" that require certain things of a homeowner – for example, a certain type of roof shingles may be required or garages may not be allowed to face onto a street.

Covenant has a much deeper meaning in the Bible.

Very specifically, covenants differ from contracts in these important ways:

• **No Expiration Date.** Contracts have dates of expiration. Covenants do not.

• **Vows vs. Performance Based.** Contracts are built on a foundation of performance — each person agreeing to do certain things. Covenants are held together by vows, and very specifically, they are framed and formed by a vow that God makes regarding mankind.

In contracts, what one person does can impact what another person does. In covenant, God never bases His promise on what man does, but rather, He bases His covenant solely upon Himself and His nature. God is motivated by His own love and character to make and keep the vows by which He enters covenant.

Furthermore, a contract "binds" or "releases" a commitment depending upon performance. If one person fails to uphold a contract, the other can be released from it. In covenant, a person is bound by his own word. Keeping a covenant is not a matter of what the other person does or does not do.

Let me give you an example of this. If I contract with you to do a particular task for $30 a week, I will pay you the $30 if you perform the task. No performance, no money.

But if I make a covenant vow to give you $30 a week, I must give you the $30 regardless of whether you do any tasks or not. My vow is to you, regardless of your behavior. My word and my commitment to keeping my word are what hold me to do my part in the covenant. It doesn't matter if you hurt me, become my enemy, walk away from me, or are unable to fulfill your part of the covenant. I am still bound by my vow.

• **Relationship vs. Rules Oriented.** Contracts are the sum total of "conditions" to which both parties agree. Covenants may have some conditions attached to parts of them, but the relationship that binds two parties together in a covenant is the far greater concern.

God's Covenants with His People

The first mention of covenant is in Genesis 6–9 where God initiated a covenant with Noah. This was an unconditional covenant agreement in which God took all the initiative, and in which God required no conditions or behavior on the part of man. God declared:

Behold, I establish my covenant with you, and with your seed after you;

And with every living creature that is with you, of the fowl, of the cattle, and of every beast of the earth with you; from all that go out of the ark, to every beast of the earth.

And I will establish my covenant with you; neither shall all flesh be cut off any more by the waters of a flood; neither shall there any more be a flood to destroy the earth

Genesis 9:9-11

It hasn't mattered *what* man has done toward God or against God, God has remained true to His covenant vow. Since Noah, no flood has destroyed the entire earth, cutting off all flesh.

God made a number of covenant vows to Abraham.

In Genesis 15:18, we read,

In the same day the Lord made a covenant with Abram, saying, Unto thy seed have I given this land, from the river of Egypt unto the great river, the river Euphrates.

God extended His covenant in Genesis 17:2–8. As you read through these verses, take special note of the very specific things that God promised to Abram –

And I will make my covenant between me and thee, and will multiply thee exceedingly.

And Abram fell on his face: and God talked with him, saying,

As for me, behold, my covenant is with thee, and thou shalt be a father of many nations.

Neither shall thy name any more be called Abram, but thy name shall be Abraham; for a father of many nations have I made thee.

And I will make thee exceeding fruitful, and I will make nations of thee, and kings shall come out of thee.

And I will establish my covenant between me and thee and thy seed after thee in their generations for an everlasting covenant, to be a God unto thee, and to thy seed after thee.

And I will give unto thee, and to thy seed after thee, the land wherein thou art a stranger, all the land of Canaan, for an everlasting possession; and I will be their God.

These are among the specific blessings that God vowed to Abraham:

- multiplication (children)
- father of many nations
- change of name
- exceeding fruitfulness
- kings as heirs
- land as an everlasting possession
- covenant extended to Abraham's heirs

In sum, God vowed to protect, bless, direct, watch over, prosper, heal, and multiply Abraham and those who would follow after him. God chose to align Himself with Abram. Abram did not call out to God requesting these things; rather, God chose Abram as the one whom He would bless.

Nothing on earth can compare to a covenant relationship with God! When God enters into a relationship with man, He holds nothing of Himself back. All of His promises become available. All of His presence and power can be accessed. All of His commandments are in full effect. All of His love flows freely toward that person.

At the heart of God's covenant with Abraham is relationship. God willfully chose to enter a relationship with Abraham, and He vowed that He would never abandon that relationship – either with Abraham or his heirs.

At the heart of any relationship that you or I might have with God is God's covenant – He has made a way for us to enter into a relationship with Him, and when we do, He will never abandon the relationship.

At the heart of marriage are vows rooted in covenant. They are vows that give rise to relationship. We must not abandon our covenant words, just as God never abandons His covenant with us.

A Covenant Is More than a Promise

Just as a covenant is more than contract, so it is also more than a pledge or promise.

The Hebrew word for covenant is *berith,* which means to "cut flesh or shed blood." A Bible covenant is, in truth, a blood covenant – a vow or promise that has been sealed by the shedding of blood. In the Scriptures, these vows are sometimes called "solemn vows" or a "solemn agreement." Since blood is the symbol for life, a covenant that is established with the shedding of blood is a vow or covenant that is sealed with the most precious commodity known to man and the one that most clearly signifies the totality of existence.

Berith is the word most often used in the Bible in relationship to covenant. It is the word related to the very divisions of our Christian Bibles. "Old Testament" and New "Testament" are more precisely translated as "Old Covenant" and "New Covenant." In the old covenant, the blood that was shed was that of sacrificial animals. In the new covenant, the blood that was shed was that of Jesus Christ on the cross of Calvary.

Blood Covenant Is as Old as History

The concept of covenant actually goes back to the dawn of history. Evidence of blood-related rituals and vows has been found among many ancient peoples and in the remains of civilizations on every continent. When journalist Henry Stanley went in search of Dr. Livingstone, a missionary explorer to Africa, he searched diligently but in vain until he "cut a covenant" with the chief of a significant tribe. During the ritual, each man cut his wrist and let a drop of blood fall into a glass of wine, where their blood mingled. Stanley and this chief became, in effect, "blood brothers."

To seal the covenant, the chief asked Stanley for his goat. Since Stanley was unable to digest anything other than goat's milk, the loss of the goat could have meant the loss of his own life. Nevertheless, he exchanged the goat for a metal spear. Word quickly spread through the native tribes that the "bearer of the spear" needed goat's milk and from that day, he had plenty to drink, no matter in what part of Africa he traveled. To harass anyone associated with Dr. Livingstone was to take on the chief of the fiercest tribe in Africa.

The covenant established was one in which each man made a solemn pledge to the other with his life. To harm one was to bring about the wrath of the other. To defraud one was to bring about the support of the other.

Even though this ritual was pagan in its nature, it points to the truth recognized intuitively by all peoples – including the American Indians, the islanders of the Pacific, the African natives, and the Oriental peoples – blood is the most sacred of all seals to any promise or agreement.

The Ritual of the Covenant

In ancient times, the rituals associated with making or "cutting" a covenant with another person were very precise. In many ways, our customs are an extension of these ancient rites.

The first act in the Hebrew ritual of entering into covenant was to take off one's coat and to hand it to the other person. The coat represented the person – this was a symbolic act of giving oneself. When a coat was handed over to another person publicly, every person who witnessed the act knew that a covenant was being formed.

Next, the parties entering into the covenant would take off

their belts. It was in the belt that the Hebrews held their weapons – knives, swords, and bows were all attached to the belt. The belt, therefore, was a strong symbol of a person's protection and personal defense. To hand over one's belt meant, "all of my ability to protect myself is at your disposal. If someone attacks you, I'll fight beside you. My preservation of my life is tied to your life and yours to mine."

The final step in entering a covenant relationship was to sacrifice an animal in a very specific way. The animal was cut down the back into two halves. These divided halves were placed directly opposite each other, with enough room between the two halves for a person to walk. The path that was created was bordered by two "walls" of blood, symbolizing death.

The ritual itself required that the two parties face each other, each person at one end of the path. They then would walk toward each other and pass each other, each person circling one half of the carcass, and come again to the point of meeting each other in the midst of the sacrifice. In doing this, they were saying, in effect, "I die to the person I was. I am no longer to be regarded as an individual person separate from you. I have walked through death and I stand ready to come alive to a new relationship. If I ever break this covenant agreement, I am willing to die."

The Hebrews pointed to the dead animal as they said, "If I ever break this covenant may God do the same to me and more." In other words, "May God slay me if I break this covenant."

Often, but not always, the two parties entering the covenant agreement would cut themselves, making a large gash in the palm of one hand. As the blood flowed down their arms, they would hold up their hands and swear allegiance to each other. (It is from this practice that we have our custom of an upraised arm as a person swears in a court of law to tell the truth.)

At other times, the Hebrews cut themselves at the wrist, then bound their wrists together so that their blood mingled while the terms of the covenant were stated aloud. As part of the ritual, each person would add to his name a part of the other's name.

To ensure that a sign of the covenant would always be visible, each party to the covenant would rub some kind of irritant into the wound that had been made so that the scar would always be visible evidence of the promise. Every time the person looked down at his hand or wrist, he saw a physical reminder of his word. Just as importantly, the scar was a sign that the person would never be alone again. Someone else would always be his "partner" if he experienced any kind of trouble.

Covenants were cut before witnesses, with an accounting of all that each person possessed. Thereafter, the material wealth of one was considered to be totally accessible by the other. Not only were resources combined, but debts were consolidated. If one person became sick and could not meet his obligations, the other would step in and help.

Covenants were also marked by the sharing of a memorial. This might be an exchange of gifts, or perhaps the raising of a heap of stones. In some places, a tree was planted as a lasting reminder of the covenant. When Jacob and Laban entered a covenant together, they raised a mound of stones and left a sign that said *mishpa,* which means, "God watch between you and me while we're parted from each other." This covenant was made not because Jacob and Laban liked each other, but because they did not trust each other and they wanted God to watch over the actions of the other in times when they were separated.

Abimelech and Abraham exchanged a flock of sheep as a memorial. Every time one of them saw the sheep of the other, he was reminded of the covenant that he had entered.

The final event associated with covenant making was a meal. Two elements were involved. First, the two shared a single piece of bread. As they tore the bread and fed each other, they said, in essence, "The sustenance of life is one between us." They then took a single cup of wine, a symbolic representation of the blood rituals they had undergone, and they drank from this one cup. In pagan cultures, blood was often added to the wine that was consumed, but because the Hebrews were not allowed by God to drink blood, the wine alone served as a symbol of the truth that life is in the blood. As they drank from the cup, they acknowledged that their life was one and that they would never again be thought of as two separate individuals.

God's Covenant Ritual with Abraham

Because we as Christians draw our "faith identity" from Abraham, the father of all who have faith, it is important that we take a look at the specific covenant God made with Abraham. The details are found in Genesis 15:1-21. This is a lengthy passage, but it includes all of the elements associated with covenant so it is worthy of a close reading.

> *After this, the word of the Lord came to Abram in a vision: "Do not be afraid, Abram. I am your shield, your very great reward."*
>
> *But Abram said, "O Sovereign Lord, what can you give me since I remain childless and the one who will inherit my estate is Eliezer of Damascus?" And Abram said, "You have given me no children; so a servant in my household will be my heir."*
>
> *Then the word of the Lord came to him: "This man will not be your heir, but a son coming from your own body*

will be your heir."

He took him outside and said, "Look up at the heavens and count the stars — if indeed you can count them." Then he said to him, "So shall your offspring be."

Abram believed the Lord, and he credited it to him as righteousness.

He also said to him, "I am the Lord, who brought you out of Ur of the Chaldeans to give you this land to take possession of it."

But Abram said, "O Sovereign Lord, how can I know that I will gain possession of it?"

So the Lord said to him, "Bring me a heifer, a goat and a ram, each three years old, along with a dove and a young pigeon."

Abram brought all these to him, cut them in two and arranged the halves opposite each other; the birds, however, he did not cut in half.

Then birds of prey came down on the carcasses, but Abram drove them away.

As the sun was setting, Abram fell into a deep sleep, and thick and dreadful darkness came over him.

Then the Lord said to him, "Know for certain that your descendants will be strangers in a country not their own, and they will be enslaved and mistreated four hundred years.

But I will punish the nation they serve as slaves, and

afterward they will come out with great possessions.

You, however, will go to your fathers in peace and be buried at a good old age.

In the fourth generation your descendants will come back here, for the sin of the Amorites has not yet reached its full measure."

When the sun had set and darkness had fallen, a smoking fire pot with a blazing torch appeared and passed between the pieces.

On that day the Lord made a covenant with Abram and said, "To your descendants I give this land, from the river of Egypt to the great river, the Euphrates – the land of the

Kenites, Kenizzites, Kadmonites,

Hittites, Perizzites, Rephaites,

Amorites, Canaanites, Girgashites and Jebusites"

Genesis 15:1-21
(NIV)

This chapter has so many symbols that our minds tend to be boggled. But it is out of this ritual that many of our customs related to weddings have arisen.

Note these specific elements of covenant-making:

• **Removal of Coat and Belt.** These actions, which are symbolic of one's identity and provision, are in place when God says, "Do not be afraid, Abram. I am your shield, your very great reward."

God is the source of all good gifts. He gave Himself as the Shield and Reward. In this covenant, man is not moving toward God, but rather, God is moving toward man. In fact, Abraham brings nothing more than his barrenness – his lack of a child – to the covenant. He says, "O Sovereign Lord, what can you give me since I remain childless?"

God extends to Abraham the very provision that Abraham needs – what Abraham lacks, God provides. It is Abraham's belief in God's promised provision that God counts as the righteousness necessary for Abraham to become a full covenant partner.

What a wonderful picture is given for the loving way in which God deals with man! God states His promises – Abram shares his doubts. God is always a God of possibilities and of great blessing. God does not have any doubt or hesitation about His desire to bring about His best for us. In contrast, we are the ones who have doubts about the goodness of God.

• **Walls of Blood.** God instructs Abram to cut apart three animals and to bring two birds to the covenant sacrifice. Abram divides these animals as God directs, creating a pathway marked by walls of blood.

Abraham does not walk through this pathway. To do so would have been to encounter God face to face, which was always prohibited to the Hebrews. Instead of a face-to-face encounter, God causes Abraham to fall into a sleep. In a vision, Abraham sees a blazing torch and a smoking fire pot passing through the pieces. The fullness of the covenant ritual is enacted although Abraham doesn't physically participate in the event. It seems that Abraham is "seeing" someone take his place in this ceremonial event – someone is assuming his identity in the covenant ritual.

In John 8:56 we read these words of Jesus: "Your father Abraham rejoiced to see my day: and he saw it, and was glad." The clear inference is that Abraham had a vision of Jesus walking in Abraham's place through the wall of blood.

Surely the angels must have stood in wonder at that moment, incredulous that a holy God could ever come into covenant with sinful man. Man had nothing to offer God, although God had everything to offer man. This experience in the life of Abraham is one of the most holy, awesome acts of mercy in all of history.

Among the Greeks, different terms are used regarding covenant. One term is used for covenants made between equal parties, and another word is used for covenants made between partners that are unequal. The latter term applies to the type of covenant we find in Genesis 15.

If a millionaire and a beggar formed a covenant bond, the beggar would bring little but himself to the covenant. Even so, the millionaire might say, "I want this beggar friend to have access to all that is mine." The lawyers would then draw up the necessary papers, even though the agreement was clearly one-sided. It is this type of covenant that God made with mankind through Abraham.

· **Mark of Wounding.** The covenant that God struck with Abraham was sealed by the mark of circumcision in Abraham. It is a mark in the flesh that Jewish men have kept through the centuries to remind them that they are partners in the covenant of Abraham. (See Genesis 17:11–14.)

· **Name Changed.** In the seventeenth chapter of Genesis, we find that Abram's name is changed to Abraham. The Hebrews took the name of God so seriously that it was never spoken aloud. They did this out of fear that they might inadvertently take the name of God in vain. In the Greek language, therefore, the name of God is translated as having consonants with no vowels: YHWH. The "H" from this name is what God inserts into Abraham's name when He changes it from Abram to Abraham. The same letter is also added to Sarai's name to change it to Sarah.

After the covenant is sealed, God allows Himself to be referred to by later prophets as the "God of Abraham." God aligns himself with Abraham's name, just as Abraham was aligned with His own name.

· **Gifts.** God gives to Abraham the promise of land that will be his forever. God also gave to Abraham and Sarah the gift of a child through which the twelve tribes of Israel were later established.

· **Friends Forever.** One of the sure signs that the covenant was sealed between God and Abraham is that Abraham became called the "friend of God." A person could not touch Abraham after that ritual ceremony without touching God, as a number of kings and rulers of nearby areas learned in the ensuing years.

In many ways, Abraham lost his identity in the covenant. He became a man so closely associated with God that in many respects, he shared God's identity and power. He was a part of God's "family."

The Covenant and Marriage Ceremonies

These ancient Hebrew rituals run through almost every modern act of pledging loyalty that we have in our world today, and especially in our Christian ceremonies of marriage. When we take them lightly, we do ourselves damage.

In review, a covenant involves:
· The identity of one person being linked to another.
· An agreement to fight for the other in times of conflict.
· A solemn pledge sealed by blood.
· The marking of each person in the covenant in a lasting way.

- The sharing of assets and debts.
- The exchange of gifts as a memorial.
- The sharing of a covenant meal.

In Christian marriages, couples are introduced as "husband and wife," a new societal unit. The identity of husband and wife are linked inseparably with the admonition, "let no man put asunder what God has joined together." There is generally an understanding that the couple will have a shared life, including shared assets and debts. The agreement is implicit that they will uphold and defend each other "in sickness and in health, in good times and bad, until death."

In modern marriage rituals, the persons entering into the marriage covenant generally exchange rings. This is a symbolic sign that has replaced the scar on the palm or wrist as a lasting sign that both parties have entered into a covenant. In a Christian marriage, the assumption is made that both parties entering the marriage are virgins. The shedding of blood occurs at the time the marriage is consummated sexually and the woman's hymen is penetrated. (In Jewish tradition, a bloody sheet from the marriage bed was considered legal proof that the bride was a virgin at the time of her wedding.)

There is a changing of names in a marriage, and at the conclusion of the wedding ceremony, a meal is often shared – the sharing of a piece of cake and a glass of beverage is symbolic of the covenant meal. Generally, a new bride and groom exchange gifts with each other – very often a piece of jewelry or a notable possession.

In so many ways, our wedding ceremonies mirror all of the aspects related to covenant!

The Lasting Nature of Covenant

There are two additional concepts related to covenant that are worth noting in our discussion since they relate to the way in which we Christians are linked to the old covenant that God forged with Abraham. They are these:

· **Children of Covenant.** The children of those who entered into a covenant agreement – both those already born and those as yet unborn – were obligated to keep the covenant until they reached the age of personal accountability. At that point, they had to decide whether or not to enter the covenant for themselves (and for their children). This ceremony of accepting the covenant of God and its responsibilities to the broader community of faith is called the Bar Mitzvah (son of the covenant) or Bat Mitzvah (daughter of the covenant) among Jewish people. In many Christian denominations, the ceremony called confirmation is intended to serve this purpose. In other Christian denominations, children are called to make a commitment of their lives to Jesus Christ upon reaching the age of accountability.

At no time, however, is a covenant not extended as an option for the next generation. This is important for us to recognize. Although we might say today as Christians that we do not live "under the law," the provisions of the covenant still extend to us. The power of the covenant and the reality of the covenant are just as much alive today as they were in the days of Abraham. The covenant is extended to us; our part is to accept it.

· **Altering a Covenant.** The only way in which a covenant can be altered is for both parties to enter into a new covenant agreement – same ritual, but new "terms" to the covenant being spoken aloud and agreed to by both parties.

In the next chapter, we will explore how God's covenant was "altered" through Jesus Christ to become an even better covenant!

Scriptures That Confirm:

We Are Partakers in Abraham's Covenant

That in blessing I will bless thee, and in multiplying I will multiply thy seed as the stars of the heaven, and as the sand which is upon the sea shore; and thy seed shall possess the gate of his enemies;

And in thy seed shall all the nations of the earth be blessed; because thou hast obeyed my voice

Genesis 22:17-18

And I will make thy seed to multiply as the stars of heaven, and will give unto thy seed all these countries; and in thy seed shall all the nations of the earth be blessed;

Because that Abraham obeyed my voice, and kept my charge, my commandments, my statutes, and my laws

Genesis 26:4-5

Even as Abraham believed God, and it was accounted to him for righteousness.

Know ye therefore that they which are of faith, the same are the children of Abraham

Galatians 3:6-7

Christ hath redeemed us from the curse of the law, being made a curse for us: for it is written, Cursed is every one that hangeth on a tree;

That the blessing of Abraham might come on the Gentiles through Jesus Christ; that we might receive the promise of the Spirit through faith

Galatians 3:13-14

Chapter 3

Chapter 3

Our Covenant in Christ Jesus

Many of us, it seems, come to Christ almost in spite of what we have been taught about God. Early in our lives we were told the many rules and regulations related to God – all of the do's and don'ts, places we could and could not go, things we could and could not do – and in our spirits, we had a great sense of obligation, a feeling of "have to" associated with God. Becoming a religious person seemed, to us, to be like walking a high wire, always tentative in our balance and fearful of falling away from God.

Then we heard the Gospel, which literally means "good news!" We learned that a new covenant had been made between God and man. The old rules and regulations were not the total story – God was going to do something in our hearts that would cause us to want to obey God from the inside out. Furthermore, the new covenant was based on what God had done for us, not on what we were being required to do for Him. The terms of covenant ultimately required our obedience and faithfulness, but the sacrifice associated with the covenant was one that did not need to be repeated. What good news, indeed!

The new covenant was, and is, one that God has made through the shed blood of Jesus Christ.

Always, we must recognize that Jesus is God's gift to us – as John 3:16 says, "God so loved the world that he *gave*." God took the initiative in sending Jesus to us. The covenant He makes through the shed blood of Jesus Christ is an extension and an elaboration of the covenant He made with Abraham – it is the *fulfillment* of that covenant.

Also, as is true of all God-initiated covenants, we must recognize that we can never deserve all of the blessings associated with the covenant that God offers through Jesus Christ. Nevertheless, we have been given the privilege to believe for and to receive the blessings of the covenant. (In like manner, your spouse may not deserve all of the blessings of living in a covenant relationship with you, but nevertheless, you have the privilege of granting to your spouse, out of your own generous love and mercy, the blessings and gifts of your time, service, and affection.)

The apostle Paul clearly described our unworthiness to receive from God, writing, "Not by works of righteousness which we have done, but according to his mercy he saved us, by the washing of regeneration, and renewing of the Holy Ghost" (Titus 3:5).

A Difference in Our Response

The covenant that God made through Jesus Christ did not differ in quality or function from that which God made with Abraham. Rather, it differs in what we must do in order to come into alignment with the covenant agreement. Under the terms of the Old Covenant (or Old Testament), the sacrifice of sheep and other animals was required to renew the covenant. In the New Covenant (or New Testament), the sacrifice made by Jesus was a one-time, never-needs-to-be-repeated sacrifice for all who believe.

The writer to the Hebrews quotes the prophet Jeremiah who foresaw and spoke about the new covenant that we have as Christians –

God found fault with the people and said: "The time is coming, declares the Lord, when I will make a new covenant with the house of Israel and with the house of Judah.

It will not be like the covenant I made with their forefathers when I took them by the hand to lead them out of Egypt, because they did not remain faithful to my covenant, and I turned away from them, declares the Lord.

This is the covenant I will make with the house of Israel after that time, declares the Lord. I will put my laws in their minds and write them on their hearts. I will be their God, and they will be my people.

No longer will a man teach his neighbor, or a man his brother, saying, 'Know the Lord,' because they will all know me, from the least of them to the greatest.

For I will forgive their wickedness and will remember their sins no more."

By calling this covenant "new," he has made the first one obsolete; and what is obsolete and aging will soon disappear

Hebrews 8:8-13
(NIV)

Jesus Fulfilled All Aspects of Covenant

Let us note very briefly the ways in which Jesus fulfilled all aspects associated with blood covenant:

- **No Expiration Date.** Christ died once and for all mankind.

(See Romans 6:10 and Hebrews 10:10–14.) The covenant God made through Jesus Christ is in effect.

· **Vows.** When we receive Christ, we are to confess Him as Lord. Romans 10:9 tells us, "If thou shalt confess with thy mouth the Lord Jesus, and shalt believe in thine heart that God hath raised him from the dead, thou shalt be saved." In 1 John 4:15 we find an echo of this idea: "Whosoever shall confess that Jesus is the Son of God, God dwelleth in him, and he in God."

Furthermore, Jesus said, "Whosoever shall confess me before men, him shall the Son of man also confess before the angels of God" (Luke 12:8).

· **Removal of Coat and Belt.** Jesus died naked upon the cross in order that He might become our full provision and source of protection against all evil. He humbled Himself to become man, so that He might lead us to a victorious life. In coming to the earth as the incarnate Son of God, Jesus gave up every vestige of heavenly prestige and honor that He had. (See Philippians 2:8.)

· **Walls of Blood.** Jesus was not only wounded with the lashes from a severe scourging – a form of Roman torture that would have deeply gashed His back – but He was crucified by having His hands and feet nailed to a cross. His side was pierced with a spear. Jesus shed all of His blood for us. (See Matthew 26:28.)

How beautiful and awe inspiring are the words of Isaiah 53 in the light of covenant. Not only did Jesus give us access to His name and power, but He literally took our place in judgment –

He is despised and rejected of men; a man of sorrows, and acquainted with grief: and we hid as it were our faces from him; he was despised, and we esteemed him not.

Surely he hath borne our griefs, and carried our sorrows:

yet we did esteem him stricken, smitten of God, and afflicted.

But he was wounded for our transgressions, he was bruised for our iniquities: the chastisement of our peace was upon him; and with his stripes we are healed.

All we like sheep have gone astray; we have turned every one to his own way; and the Lord hath laid on him the iniquity of us all.

He was oppressed, and he was afflicted, yet he opened not his mouth: he is brought as a lamb to the slaughter, and as a sheep before her shearers is dumb, so he openeth not his mouth

Isaiah 53:3-7

The word used to describe God's work on man's behalf is "grace." A well-known phrase has made GRACE an acronym standing for:

G - God's
R - riches
A - at
C - Christ's
E - expense

All that God possesses, He has made available to us through the shed blood of Jesus Christ. Jesus paid the debt for our sins *in full.* Salvation from sin's penalty of death is offered to us as a free gift. All that is required is that we believe.

No person can come to God on the basis of what he or she has done, said, accomplished, earned, or achieved. Rather, we come into relationship with God on the basis of our believing in what Jesus Christ has done – that He has paid in full the penalty for sin through His sacrificial death.

· **Mark of Wounding.** The scars on Jesus' side and wrists are the mark of Christ's covenant with us. The covenant He makes with us is sealed by the Holy Spirit, who comes to dwell within us when we receive the forgiveness that God offers to us through Christ's sacrificial death. In the Holy Spirit, we are marked as Christ's own forever.

Rather than seek a bodily circumcision, God requires of us a "circumcised heart" – a heart that has been changed by the power of the Holy Spirit. As Colossians 2:11,13 says, "In whom also ye are circumcised with the circumcision made without hands, in putting off the body of the sins of the flesh by the circumcision of Christ: . . . and you, being dead in your sins and the uncircumcision of your flesh, hath he quickened together with him, having forgiven you all trespasses."

· **Change of Name.** The Bible speaks repeatedly of the new identity we have in Christ. Indeed, when we call ourselves Christians we are taking on the name of Christ! In Revelation we read about the new name that Christ gives to us: "To him that overcometh will I give to eat of the hidden manna, and will give him a white stone, and in the stone a new name written, which no man knoweth saving he that receiveth it" (Revelation 2:17).

· **Gifts.** In establishing covenant with God through Jesus Christ, we not only receive the free gift of redemption from sin and the gift of everlasting life, but we also receive the gifts that come with the presence of the Holy Spirit indwelling us. (See John 3:16, Romans 5:15, 1 Corinthians 12.) In fact, the Bible tells us that every good and perfect gift is from God and is made available to us through Jesus Christ. (See James 1:17.)

· **Forever Friends.** The covenant relationship we have with Jesus Christ will last forever. God has promised us an eternal reign with Jesus. (See Hebrews 5:9 and Hebrews 9:12.)

In all ways Jesus fulfilled perfectly the covenant relationship God had established with Abraham, yet with two marked differences:

First, the old covenant bears a feeling of "have to." The new covenant in Christ Jesus births within us a desire of "want to." The person who is in genuine covenant relationship with Christ Jesus *wants* to serve God and to obey God's commandments.

Second, the old covenant required outward, visible, sacrificial acts of repentance. The new covenant requires only that we believe – that we confess to God our sinful nature and receive the forgiveness God so freely offers to us. The only sacrifice we are called to make is a sacrifice of praise and thanksgiving. The foremost outward signs required of us are baptism and an open confession of Christ with our words and our lives.

Covenant Power for Our Marriages

The covenant power that binds us to Christ is available to us as the binding force of our marriages.

It is Christ dwelling in us who enables us to enter into a covenant relationship with another person, so that we will have marriages that do not have "expiration dates." It is Christ who enables us to make a vow and keep it. It is Christ who empowers us to build a relationship in which we protect and provide for another person in marriage. It is Christ who helps us adopt and live in a "married" identity. It is Christ who gives us His gifts to bestow upon our marriage partner. It is Christ who abides in our marriage with us.

The covenant of Abraham and the covenant of Jesus – in substance and quality, one covenant – extend to our marriages because Christ dwells within us and we in Him. When two people dwell in Christ individually and then come together in marriage, they dwell in Christ together as husband and wife. They are one in flesh – one entity before God. They are bound in covenant to Christ no longer as individuals alone, but as individuals united in marriage.

Scriptures That Confirm:

We Are Heirs to the Covenant

The following verses underscore our identity in Christ as children of God the Father. As you read through them, reflect upon what a blessing has been given to you that you might be called a covenant child of the Heavenly Father!

[Jesus said], "But I say unto you, Love your enemies, bless them that curse you, do good to them that hate you, and pray for them which despitefully use you, and persecute you;

that ye may be the children of your Father which is in heaven"

Matthew 5:44-45

[Jesus said], "But love ye your enemies, and do good, and lend, hoping for nothing again; and your reward shall be great, and ye shall be the children of the Highest: for he is kind unto the unthankful and to the evil"

Luke 6:35

[Jesus said], "But as many as received him, to them gave he power to become the sons of God, even to them that believe on his name:

which were born, not of blood, nor of the will of the flesh, nor of the will of man, but of God"

John 1:12-13

It was not through law that Abraham and his offspring received the promise that he would be heir of the world, but through the righteousness that comes by faith.

For if those who live by law are heirs, faith has no value and the promise is worthless,

because law brings wrath. And where there is no law there is no transgression.

Therefore, the promise comes by faith, so that it may be by grace and may be guaranteed to all Abraham's offspring – not only to those who are of the law but also to those who are of the faith of Abraham. He is the father of us all

Romans 4:13-16 (NIV)

For as many as are led by the Spirit of God, they are the sons of God.

For ye have not received the spirit of bondage again to fear; but ye have received the Spirit of adoption, whereby we cry, Abba, Father.

The Spirit itself beareth witness with our spirit, that we are the children of God:

and if children, then heirs; heirs of God, and joint-heirs with Christ; if so be that we suffer with him, that we may be also glorified together.

For I reckon that the sufferings of this present time are not worthy to be compared with the glory which shall be revealed in us.

For the earnest expectation of the creature waiteth for the manifestation of the sons of God

Romans 8:14-19

For from the very beginning God decided that those who came to him – and all along he knew who would – should become like his Son, so that his Son would be the First, with many brothers

Romans 8:29
(TLB)

For ye are all the children of God by faith in Christ Jesus.

For as many of you as have been baptized into Christ have put on Christ.

There is neither Jew nor Greek, there is neither bond nor free, there is neither male nor female: for ye are all one in Christ Jesus.

And if ye be Christ's, then are ye Abraham's seed, and heirs according to the promise

Galatians 3:26-29

When You Say I Do. God Says I Will

To redeem them that were under the law, that we might receive the adoption of sons.

And because ye are sons, God hath sent forth the Spirit of his Son into your hearts, crying, Abba, Father.

Wherefore thou art no more a servant, but a son; and if a son, then an heir of God through Christ

Galatians 4:5-7

His unchanging plan has always been to adopt us into his own family by sending Jesus Christ to die for us. And he did this because he wanted to!

Ephesians 1:5 (TLB)

Now all of us, whether Jews or Gentiles, may come to God the Father with the Holy Spirit's help because of what Christ has done for us.

Now you are no longer strangers to God and foreigners to heaven, but you are members of God's very own family, citizens of God's country, and you belong in God's household with every other Christian.

What a foundation you stand on now: the apostles and the prophets; and the cornerstone of the building is Jesus Christ himself!

We who believe are carefully joined together with Christ as parts of a beautiful, constantly growing temple for God.

And you also are joined with him and with each other by the Spirit and are part of this dwelling place of God

Ephesians 2:18-22
(TLB)

That ye may be blameless and harmless, the sons of God, without rebuke, in the midst of a crooked and perverse nation, among whom ye shine as lights in the world

Philippians 2:15

Chapter 4

CHAPTER 4

God's Strength and Provision for Our Weakness and Need

Keeping covenant with God allows a person to do any number of things they would not normally be able to do in their own strength. This is illustrated in King David's life.

We are drawn to David not because of his perfection – in truth, he was blatantly human and failed horribly on a number of occasions – but because he lived his life fully and was resolute in his trust of God. David understood and kept covenant with God.

You Do Not Go into Battle Alone

One of the great provisions of covenant, as we have discussed previously, is that God extends all of His omnipotence and omnipresence to us. We are never alone. We are always "in Christ."

The provision of God's powerful presence was certainly something that David knew, and upon which he relied. When David came to the battlefield in 1 Samuel 17, he found the army of Israel confused and afraid. Goliath was mocking the people of God. David asked, "Who is this uncircumcised Philistine that he should defy the armies of the living God?" David perceived only two types of people – God's people and all others. Since God's people bore the mark of the covenant in circumcision, David was stating boldly that Goliath was "outside the covenant," an enemy of Israel but even more importantly, an enemy of God.

David's battle cry confirms his belief about Goliath as God's enemy. As he raced down into the valley to confront Goliath, David cried, "Thou comest to me with a sword, and with a spear, and with a shield: but I come to thee in the name of the Lord of hosts, the God of the armies of Israel, whom thou hast defied. . . . And all this assembly shall know that the Lord saveth not with sword and spear: for the battle is the Lord's, and he will give you into our hands" (1 Samuel 17:45,47).

Armed with only a slingshot and rushing toward a battle with a giant warrior, David must have appeared a madman to the other Israelites. What they could not see, and did not understand, was that David knew he had Almighty God as a covenant partner in the battle against Goliath.

Every Israelite within the range of David's voice that day was a participant in the covenant God had made with Abraham. They had the promise, but not the faith to act on the promise. David had the faith. He had learned to exercise his faith through prior experiences of trusting God to help him defeat both a lion and bear. The confidence David took with him into battle was not ill-founded. He was trusting in the One who had been faithful to deliver him in the past.

There are times when discussions that arise from marital difficulties may seem like a battlefield. As you go into those discussions – perhaps with your spouse privately, in a counseling session, in the presence of attorneys, or even in court – go with the full understanding that you are in covenant with God. You do not enter any situation alone.

No matter how small or vulnerable you may feel, and no matter how others may perceive you, you are inseparably linked with the Almighty. Do not trust in yourself alone. Trust in God!

Our Position Is Always Vulnerable

We must never lose sight of the fact that we are in a vulnerable position on this earth, regardless of how much earthly power or security we seem to have acquired in the eyes of our fellow man. We are not omnipotent – rather, we are very weak in comparison to nature's forces. Even among the creatures of the earth, we are by no means the fastest, strongest, or biggest. We crumble when infected by viruses and bacteria that cannot even be seen by the human eye!

Not only are we vulnerable in many ways physically, but we also live in a world in which we are very vulnerable politically. We like to think we live in an era of peace, yet wars are raging all around us – and sometimes in neighborhoods very close to ours – at all times. Furthermore, we are always vulnerable to spiritual attack, no matter how long we have been a Christian or how strong we are in faith.

Abraham was in a vulnerable position as well. Alone and wandering with his family and associates in a land that wasn't his own, he was subject to all forms of danger and temptation. Yet it is in this very environment that God moved toward him to forge covenant.

In covenant lie help and security. Time and again through the Scriptures we find that covenant is linked with the concept of help, salvation, or deliverance. Zacharias, the father of John the Baptist, aptly described man's condition as he foresaw the coming of Christ –

> *Blessed be the Lord God of Israel; for he hath visited and redeemed his people, . . .*
>
> *that we should be saved from our enemies, and from the hand of all that hate us:*

to perform the mercy promised to our fathers, and to remember his holy covenant, . . .

that he would grant unto us, that we being delivered out of the hand of our enemies might serve him without fear, . . .

to give light to them that sit in darkness and in the shadow of death, to guide our feet into the way of peace

Luke 1:68,71-72,74,79

The enemy of our souls is, of course, our foremost enemy. He deceives, accuses, tempts, and lies. (See 2 Corinthians 11:3, Revelation 12:10, Matthew 4:1, and John 8:44.) He is a thief, a murderer, and a destroyer. (See John 10:10.) Furthermore, he has great power. (See 2 Corinthians 4:4.) It is no wonder that Peter said, "Be sober, be vigilant; because your adversary the devil, as a roaring lion, walketh about, seeking whom he may devour" (1 Peter 5:8.)

Man desperately needs God's protection!

Our Provision Is Certain

The good news of the Bible is that God has generously made such protection available to us through our covenant relationship with Jesus Christ. Even as Paul cautioned about the devil's power, he also pointed toward the provision made for us through relationship with Christ –

For we wrestle not against flesh and blood, but against principalities, against powers, against the rulers of the darkness of this world, against spiritual wickedness in high places.

Wherefore take unto you the whole armor of God, that ye

may be able to withstand in the evil day, and having done all, to stand

Ephesians 6:12-13

The armor that Paul describes is not physical or material armor – neither is it political, financial, or an armor forged in alliances with other people. The armor is spiritual – it is the very nature of Christ Jesus manifest in us. Our armor is a breastplate of righteousness, a shield of faith, a helmet of salvation, a girdle of truth, shoes of the preparation of the Gospel of peace, and a sword of the Spirit which is the Word of God. We are to clothe ourselves in relationship with Jesus Christ and speak His words to our enemy, even as we remain diligent in prayer. That is the stance we are to take in order to put ourselves into a position of safety and security in Christ.

When Arlene was threatened with divorce by her husband, she literally obeyed the command of Paul to the Ephesians. She recognized that the devil was after her marriage and her witness to others. She began each day with prayer, and as if miming the act of "dressing herself" in armor, she declared to God that she was putting on the armor that He had provided to her. She would say aloud, "I am putting on the girdle of truth today. I will take strength in the truth of God's Word and I will choose to believe only what God says about me, my marriage, and my future with my husband." She would say, "I am taking up the shield of faith today. I will not be intimidated by the enemy or give in to fear. I will speak God's Word directly into the face of any threat or any confusion that the devil sends my way." She made a similar statement regarding each of the pieces of armor described in Ephesians 6:14-18 –

- loins girt about with truth
- breastplate of righteousness
- feet shod with the preparation of the gospel of peace
- shield of faith, wherewith ye shall be able to quench all

of the fiery darts of the wicked
- helmet of salvation
- sword of the Spirit, which is the Word of God

Arlene also took seriously the words of Paul that she was to "stand" in her armor, firm in her position that God would intervene on her behalf. Paul wrote in Ephesians 6:13, "Wherefore take unto you the whole armor of God, that ye may be able to withstand in the evil day, and having done all, to stand." Arlene saw her position as one of a strong defense, not an offense. Although her friends were quick to suggest that she seek out legal counsel or even that she grant her husband the divorce he sought, she remained firm in her position. She would simply say, "No, I'm choosing to stand in faith that God will win this assault against our marriage and that our relationship will emerge even stronger than before."

When her husband brought up the subject of divorce, Arlene would respond to him by saying, "I am praying and believing that God will change your heart regarding this and will reveal to you how much He loves you and how much I love you. Our marriage is worth fighting for and I'm going to fight for it in prayer."

Arlene was consistent in her waging of this spiritual battle for her marriage. She refused to give in to the threat of divorce, even when she felt weak, discouraged, or depressed at her husband's seemingly equal resolve to end their twenty-year marriage.

After five months of daily putting on the armor of God and standing in faith, Arlene's husband came to her one day and said, "The Lord really got my attention last night and He showed me that I have been pursuing the wrong path. He told me that I should start putting the same amount of energy and effort into improving our marriage that I've been putting into a divorce."

Arlene, of course, was delighted! She heartily agreed to do her part in improving areas of their marriage relationship that had been neglected or which had become weakened through the years.

Five years later, Arlene's husband said to her, "The more I wanted divorce, the more you stood in faith for our marriage. I saw a new strength in you I hadn't seen before. I saw how important our marriage was to you, and also how much you valued being with me. I thought to myself, Where am I going to find another woman that wants so much to be married to me? I decided I probably wouldn't find such a woman. It's at that point that God really began to work in my heart."

When we remain true to the covenant we have with God, He keeps us under His cover of protection. No wonder David was able to proclaim with such joy –

> *Bless the Lord, O my soul: and all that is within me, bless his holy name.*
>
> *Bless the Lord, O my soul, and forget not all his benefits:*
>
> *Who forgiveth all thine iniquities; who healeth all thy diseases;*
>
> *Who redeemeth thy life from destruction; who crowneth thee with lovingkindness and tender mercies:*
>
> *Who satisfieth thy mouth with good things; so that thy youth is renewed like the eagle's.*
>
> *The Lord executeth righteousness and judgment for all that are oppressed*
>
> Psalm 103:1-6

As Christians, the will of God for us is sure. He desires only good things for His people. At the same time, He commands that we remain faithful to our relationship with Him. We are never without help in our fight to remain true to our commitments.

God Never Forgets His Covenant with Us

Time and time again, the Israelites fell into sinful patterns, even to the point of worshipping false gods and moving away from the covenant they once had made with God. When the consequences of their sin began to pile high enough to cause them great pain and suffering, they invariably turned back to God, praying, "O God, remember the covenant You made with our father Abraham." Although the Israelites wavered in their obedience to God, they never wavered in their belief that God would be true to the covenant He had made.

One such time occurred when the Israelites found themselves slaves in Egypt and we are told that God "remembered the covenant" and put His hand on Moses, calling him to take the lead in freeing God's people from bondage.

We each find ourselves in this position when we come to Christ: we have done nothing to earn God's forgiveness and deliverance. Even so, as a child of God and the recipient of God's great mercy, we are given every right to release our faith in Him and to see God work great miracles on our behalf.

Those miracles include the healing of our marriages, our relationships with our children and with others, our finances, and every other aspect of our lives.

Like Moses, we often have great doubts about our abilities. Moses adopted this stance in the face of God's calling: "I can't do this." God responded, in essence, saying, "I know you can't; I can and I will. I will bring about the release of My people. They are Mine, not yours. Your job is to go and speak to Pharaoh. My job is to free My people."

Moses obeyed. Again and again, he confronted Pharaoh with the demand, "The One God, Jehovah, says, 'Let My people go.'" Pharaoh denied the release of the Hebrews and time and again, God showed His awesome power until the nation was devastated and plundered. Moses, and the people themselves, had done nothing to win their release. God had done it all!

The problems only multiplied as Moses led the people away from Egypt and toward the land God had promised to them. Again and again, they faced problems related to what they would eat, drink, and wear. When these problems arose, Moses went to God saying, "God, You have a problem." He was a firm believer in the covenant — he did not perceive the problems to be his alone. He was in covenant with God! And each time, God gave Moses specific instructions about what God had chosen as a course of action.

God supplied His people with manna, water, health, clothing that didn't wear out, and a law to unify and direct their moral lives. He led them with a pillar of fire at night and a pillar of cloud by day. These miracles not only gave direction, but comfort. In all ways, God proved Himself to be their Shield and Provision.

When the Israelites entered combat with the Amalekites as they wandered in the wilderness, God provided the victory. The battle was won not on the basis of Joshua's leadership or upon the superior weapons or fighting skills of the Israelites, but rather, upon whether Moses' hands remained lifted up in worship and surrender to God the Deliverer.

For forty years, God showed Himself strong on behalf of His people, leading them and teaching them until they were prepared to "take" the land He had promised to them. And even at that point, the miracles continued. God promised them great harvests, great flocks, immeasurable wealth, and that they would be the head and not the tail. Walking in covenant, the Israelites put their feet in the Jordan River and it parted. Walking in covenant, they marched around the city of Jericho in obedience to God's instructions, and God caused the city walls to fall. At one time, God even threw hailstones out of heaven to defeat their enemies. Time and again, story after story, incident after incident, God showed His power on behalf of the people with whom He had a covenant agreement.

The result was that a broken and enslaved people became a great people, a people that conquered and flourished and planted and reaped in abundance. God was true to His covenant promises even when the Israelites turned away from Him. Those who had a clear understanding of covenant knew fully that the victory and the strength of the Israelites rested solely in God.

When King Jehoshaphat found himself in a situation where three nations had teamed up against him and had surrounded Jerusalem with their armies, Jehoshaphat turned to God. He reminded God of the promise He had made to Abraham and of His prevailing goodness in upholding the covenant. Jahaziel then prophesied back to Jehoshaphat, "The battle is not yours but the Lord's." (See 2 Chronicles 20.)

That is always the stance we have in the covenant. The battle is not ours alone. There is a part for us to play. But ultimately, the battle is the Lord's. The victory is His.

Jehoshaphat was so confident in the prophecy from Jahaziel that he put the choir in front of the army as they marched out to do battle the next day. At the end of the day, the enemy had been defeated without a single loss of life to the Israelites. In the aftermath of the fighting – one invading army fighting the other invading armies – all that remained for the Israelites to do was to collect the booty left behind!

This, too, is a clear picture of our response to the God of covenant who fights and wins battles on our behalf. Our part is to praise God – with shouts and songs of high acclaim – and then to trust God with the full victory. When the battle is over and the victory has been claimed, we will always find an overflowing blessing available for the "gathering" by those who have trusted God without wavering.

King Hezekiah also faced a potential disaster. Sennacherib showed up outside Jerusalem and laid siege to the city, calling out intimidating taunts and claiming that all of the gods of other nations had failed against the might of Babylon. Israel was out-armed and outmanned. In fact, the Israelites hardly had anything that even could be considered an army. Hezekiah had nowhere to turn except to the promise of the covenant that God had made with Abraham and with his heirs. He went before God and voiced all of the things that were being stated against God. God told him to go home and go to sleep.

That very night, one angel killed 186,000 enemy soldiers. The God of Abraham had once again proven Himself to be the strong and powerful victor!

The message to us over and over and over throughout the Scriptures is this: the God with whom we are in covenant is more powerful than anything that the devil or evil man might do, say, or plot against us.

No matter what situation you may be in today, God is the source of your protection and your provision. He can more than compensate for any weakness or need that you are experiencing. In fact, His pledge to you in covenant relationship is that you will not only "get by," but you will move into an abundance of all things that are desirable and for your eternal benefit. God will not only keep you safe from the enemy of your soul, but He will give you victory over Satan. He is a God of triumph and giver of blessings!

Trust God today not only to be with you in times of trouble, but to be with you all the way through the trouble to a position of strength and wholeness.

Scriptures That Confirm:

God Protects and Provides

If thou wilt diligently hearken to the voice of the Lord thy God, and wilt do that which is right in his sight, and wilt give ear to his commandments, and keep all his statutes, I will put none of these diseases upon thee, which I have brought upon the Egyptians: for I am the Lord that healeth thee

Exodus 15:26

The Lord is my shepherd; I shall not want.

He maketh me to lie down in green pastures: he leadeth me beside the still waters.

He restoreth my soul: he leadeth me in the paths of righteousness for his name's sake.

Yea, though I walk through the valley of the shadow of death, I will fear no evil: for thou art with me; thy rod and thy staff they comfort me.

Thou preparest a table before me in the presence of mine enemies: thou anointest my head with oil; my cup runneth over.

Surely goodness and mercy shall follow me all the days of my life: and I will dwell in the house of the Lord for ever

Psalm 23:1-6

Blessed be the Lord, who daily loadeth us with benefits, even the God of our salvation

Psalm 68:19

He that dwelleth in the secret place of the most High shall abide under the shadow of the Almighty.

I will say of the Lord, He is my refuge and my fortress: my God; in him will I trust.

Surely he shall deliver thee from the snare of the fowler, and from the noisome pestilence.

He shall cover thee with his feathers, and under his wings shalt thou trust: his truth shall be thy shield and buckler.

Thou shalt not be afraid for the terror by night; nor for the arrow that flieth by day;

nor for the pestilence that walketh in darkness; nor for the destruction that wasteth at noonday.

A thousand shall fall at thy side, and ten thousand at thy right hand; but it shall not come nigh thee.

Only with thine eyes shalt thou behold and see the reward of the wicked.

Because thou hast made the Lord, which is my refuge,

even the most High, thy habitation;

there shall no evil befall thee, neither shall any plague come nigh thy dwelling.

For he shall give his angels charge over thee, to keep thee in all thy ways.

They shall bear thee up in their hands, lest thou dash thy foot against a stone.

Thou shalt tread upon the lion and adder: the young lion and the dragon shalt thou trample under feet.

Because he hath set his love upon me, therefore will I deliver him: I will set him on high, because he hath known my name.

He shall call upon me, and I will answer him: I will be with him in trouble; I will deliver him, and honour him. With long life will I satisfy him, and shew him my salvation

Psalm 91

Bless the Lord, O my soul: and all that is within me, bless his holy name.

Bless the Lord, O my soul, and forget not all his benefits:

who forgiveth all thine iniquities; who healeth all thy diseases;

who redeemeth thy life from destruction; who crowneth thee with lovingkindness and tender mercies;

who satisfieth thy mouth with good things; so that thy youth is renewed like the eagle's

Psalm 103:1-5

Therefore take no thought, saying, What shall we eat? or, What shall we drink? or, Wherewithal shall we be clothed?

(For after all these things do the Gentiles seek:) for your heavenly Father knoweth that ye have need of all these things.

But seek ye first the kingdom of God, and his righteousness; and all these things shall be added unto you.

Take therefore no thought for the morrow: for the morrow shall take thought for the things of itself. Sufficient unto the day is the evil thereof.

Matthew 6:31-34

Now I entrust you to God and his care and to his wonderful words which are able to build your faith and give you all the inheritance of those who are set apart for himself

Acts 20:32 (TLB)

My God shall supply all your need according to his riches in glory by Christ Jesus

Philippians 4:19

(For the weapons of our warfare are not carnal, but mighty through God to the pulling down of strong holds;)

casting down imaginations, and every high thing that exalteth itself against the knowledge of God, and bringing into captivity every thought to the obedience of Christ

2 Corinthians 10:4-5

Chapter 5

CHAPTER 5

God Gives Us His Name as Our Indentity (Part 1)

An important aspect of covenant is the taking on of the name of the person with whom you are in covenant. Names are of great significance, both in the ancient world and today. To know the name of another person is truly to begin to know that person; to take on the name of another person is to take on the characteristics and qualities associated with that person.

In Bible times, especially, to know another person's name was a privilege that offered access to that person's thoughts, personality, and life. Names had great meaning. They were a verbal embodiment of the "whole" of the person. To know a person's name was a necessary ingredient to having a relationship with a person, and also a prerequisite if one desired to have authority over that person. Those without known names fell into the nebulous category of "stranger."

God favored His people by revealing Himself to them through various names. Each name offered insight into His love and righteousness. God's revelation of His names built relationship with His people.

We certainly know the importance of names in our lives today as we relate to other human beings. We each not only have our given name but also a family name. Christensen and Griego are the families to which we belong. When a person gives his or her full name, we know not only what to call that person, but to which family the person belongs.

In addition, we have a number of titles that function as names, telling us something about a person. We learn a great deal by knowing if a person is Miss, Doctor, Mrs., Reverend, General, The Honorable, Queen, King, and so forth.

We also have titles that are linked to our family relationships. A father who calls his child "daughter" or "son" is responding to that child out of relationship.

And finally, we have nicknames. If they are affectionate names (as opposed to those rooted in ridicule or prejudice), we often respond warmly when we hear ourselves called by a nickname. There is an intimacy associated with nicknames that speaks of a special relationship.

In many ways, you are a composite of all the names and titles and nicknames that you have. If a person knows all of your names – and has a degree of understanding about why you have each name – that person will know a great deal about you! The more names, and the more intimate the names, a person has for you, the greater the bond of relationship.

What God Has Revealed through His Names

An important aspect of understanding covenant is understanding the use of "names" in a covenant. As Christians, we are privileged to use the name of the Lord as we express our faith and do what the Lord directs us to do. In 1 Samuel 17:45, David declared that he came "in the name of the Lord of hosts." David knew the name of his greatest ally and the One on whose behalf he was fighting.

One of the best ways to get to know the Lord is to study the various names that He has appropriated for Himself throughout the Scriptures. Each name reveals a unique facet of the Lord and describes one or more ways in which the Lord desires to function in relationship with us.

The Bible gives us three basic names for God. These are the names which are used the most often in Scripture. The first is *Elohim,* which means strong Creator or the Almighty. The second is *Adonai,* which means Lord or the master of a slave. The third is *Jehovah* (also translated Lord in Hebrew), which means the self-existent One who reveals Himself as a faithful covenant-keeper.

Of the three names, Jehovah is used most often in describing God's relationship to man. Various adjectives are attached to Jehovah to reveal even more aspects of His nature. Because each of these descriptive names for Jehovah is rooted in covenant, we are going to take a closer look at them to discover how our identity is to mirror that of the One with whom we are in covenant.

Jehovah-Jireh: Great Provider

In Genesis 22:14, we find Abraham in one of the most difficult tests of his life. His journey of faith had finally produced a miracle child, a son born to Abraham when Abraham was one hundred years old. Then, God asked Abraham to sacrifice that long-awaited child on an altar.

This took place at a time when people worshipped their gods with human sacrifice. Indeed, human sacrifice was not at all uncommon. Blood sacrifice was related to various rituals of "pleasing the gods" in virtually every ancient culture. What was unique about this experience with Abraham, however, was that Jehovah made it very clear to Abraham that He did not require the blood of His worshippers or their children.

God did not put this test of faith to Abraham early in their relationship. Years of relationship had passed by the time Abraham came to this point. Even so, it was a difficult challenge for Abraham. Only a man who had seen God work on his behalf time and time again could even think about going through the motions of what God had asked Abraham to do.

As Abraham raised his knife to slay his son, already bound to the altar, Abraham heard his name being called. In the next moment, he saw a ram caught in a bush. The meaning of God was clear – the ram was to be the sacrifice, not his beloved son Isaac. What joy must have filled Abraham's heart in that moment! We find this response of Abraham in Scripture –

> *Abraham called the name of that place Jehovah-jireh: as it is said to this day, in the mount of the Lord it shall be seen*
>
> Genesis 22:14

The New International Version of the Bible translates the verse this way, "So Abraham called that place 'The Lord Will Provide.' And to this day it is said, 'On the mountain of the Lord it will be provided.'"

What a wonderful expression of God to His people! Our God Jehovah will provide. He is Jehovah-Jireh, the Great Provider.

Time and again, God proved Himself to be faithful to this name. He provided a way of escape through the Red Sea. He provided land to a people without armies, water to drink in a wilderness, and above all, a Savior to completely bridge the gap between God and man that had been caused by man's sin.

God has provided for us, and as His children, we are called by Him to provide for others. Zacharias alluded to this as he prophesied the coming of Jesus –

Blessed be the Lord God of Israel; for he hath visited and redeemed his people . . .

that we should be saved from our enemies, and from the hand of all that hate us;

to perform the mercy promised to our fathers, and to remember his holy covenant;

the oath which he sware to our father Abraham,

that he would grant unto us, that we being delivered out of the hand of our enemies might serve him without fear,

in holiness and righteousness before him, all the days of our life

Luke 1:68,71-75

What Jesus does for us, we are to do for others in His name. Part of what we are called to do is to PROVIDE for others.

How does this relate to marriage?

A husband and wife are to PROVIDE for each other in a marriage relationship.

This does not mean that a husband is to provide the money and the wife is to spend it all as she desires. The provision is a two-way street. Each provides to the best of his or her ability those things which are beneficial to the marriage. If the husband is the sole provision of income, then it is the wife's responsibility to provide the maximum amount of benefit from the income – the best nutrition, the best possible environment, the best possible nurture for the children, the best possible home life.

If each person provides income to the marriage, then each is also responsible for making certain that they enjoy the maximum amount of benefit from that income – each serving the other, and both together serving the children to provide an environment that is in *every way pleasing to God.*

Notice the very specific characteristics that are identified in the prophecy of Zacharias:

• **Delivered Out of the Hand of Our Enemies.** You and your spouse are to be each other's greatest defenders – speaking well of each other, and without criticism, to any who are outside your marriage. You are to be on the alert for situations and people who might injure your spouse in some way, and to help guard your home against those who might have an ungodly influence. You are to PROVIDE for each other a strong ally, a partner in the defense of your marriage and home.

• **Serving God in Holiness and Righteousness.** You and your spouse are to create a home in which God is honored at all times and the Lord's commandments are kept by all members of the family. You are to PROVIDE for each other a place in which you both are free to worship God fully.

• **Giving Knowledge of Salvation.** You and your spouse are to remind each other, and also your children, of your complete dependence upon the saving hand of the Lord. It is the Lord who is to be praised for every act of deliverance He renders – including deliverance from evil, deliverance from difficult situations, deliverance from sickness, and deliverance from financial ruin. You are to PROVIDE for each other an environment of praise to God and an environment in which Jesus can be fully acknowledged as Savior and Lord.

• **To be a Light to Them that Sit in Darkness and in the Shadow of Death.** You and your spouse are to be good sources of truthful information to each other. This information is to be given in a way that is encouraging — which truly brings the light of knowledge but also the joy of release from something that would have been deadly to one's emotions, the marriage, a career, or one's walk with the Lord. You are to be each other's greatest fan and cheerleader. You are to PROVIDE for your spouse encouragement, inspiration, and motivation toward all that is good and of God.

• **To Guide into the Way of Peace.** You and your spouse are to create a home in which peace prevails. You are to PROVIDE for each other that safe haven at the end of the day in which each person can relax completely and enjoy fully the fellowship of being with those who love unconditionally.

We must note, of course, that there are several things that you cannot give to your spouse. Some things only God can give. You cannot give your spouse the gift of spiritual salvation — only Jesus can do that. You cannot give your spouse divine counsel for every situation of every day — only the Holy Spirit can do that. You cannot give your spouse emotional wholeness or inner healing — only Jesus the Healer can do that. You cannot be the end-all and be-all to your spouse — that is the sovereign work of God alone.

Nevertheless, we can and must give what we are capable of giving. We can do our utmost to defend our spouse, help our spouse walk in godliness, and create an atmosphere of praise and worship in the home. We can share the truth of God's Word in a loving and uplifting way. We can create an environment of peace. What wonderful provisions those are!

Furthermore, we can trust God to do in the life of our spouse what only God can do. We can believe for God to provide all that we cannot provide.

God is Jehovah-Jireh. He is our Provider. He gives what will fully equip us to be His people and to live in right relationship with Him. He is the God who is faithful and steadfast in PROVID-

ING for those with whom He has cut covenant.

If we truly are to be faithful followers and "children" of our Father who is Jehovah-Jireh, then we are to provide for others, and especially for our spouse with whom we are in covenant. Our first and foremost responsibility is to give to our spouse all that we are capable of providing and to do so with faithfulness and steadfastness.

Jehovah-Rophe: Our Healer

The second time that God linked His name to a description was shortly after Moses had led the children of Israel out of Egypt. The people had come to Marah, where they found the waters too bitter to drink. We read in Exodus 15:24-26 –

> *The people turned against Moses. "Must we die of thirst?" they demanded.*
>
> *Moses pleaded with the Lord to help them, and the Lord showed him a tree to throw into the water, and the water became sweet.*
>
> *It was there at Marah that the Lord laid before them the following conditions, to test their commitment to him: "If you will listen to the voice of the Lord your God, and obey it, and do what is right, then I will not make you suffer the diseases I send on the Egyptians, for I am the Lord who heals you"* (TLB).

Jehovah-Rophe literally means in Hebrew, "The God Who Heals."

Yes, God heals! And He is the Sustainer of health. Our healing is not only spiritual, but physical, mental, emotional, financial, and relational.

After forty years of wandering through a wilderness, the children of Israel eventually entered the land God had promised to them – they did so with full bellies and good health. The law God gave to His people was filled with commandments related not only to their physical health, but also to their social well-being. Physicians, scientists, and psychologists today have confirmed that the laws of God protect from disease and from "sick relationships" in a society. Especially in the ancient world, circumcision, not eating pork, and not drinking blood were commandments that had direct medical value.

As a part of their office, the prophets of God were given an ability to heal the sick and even to raise the dead. Jesus, too, had healing as an integral part of His ministry.

The tree which Moses cast into the waters at Marah was indicative of a much later "tree" – the cross on which Jesus was crucified in Jerusalem. Jesus was God's answer for the healing of the sin in mankind's heart. As Peter wrote about Jesus, "Who his own self bare our sins in his own body on the tree, that we, being dead to sins, should live unto righteousness" (1 Peter 2:24).

Healing involves anything that contributes to or results in wholeness – spirit, mind, body, finances, emotions, and relationships. We each are a singular entity. No one can technically divide us into spirit, mind, or body. We are an integrated whole – anything that impacts one facet of our being impacts all other facets. Therefore, healing is never just spiritual, or just physical, or just emotional. God's ultimate desire for us is that we be made whole.

As we noted in our earlier discussion of God's name of Jehovah-Jireh, we must recognize that we are individually called to be agents of healing in our world today. We are to do our utmost to help others become whole in Christ Jesus – spiritually alive through salvation and the receiving of the Holy Spirit, but also physically, emotionally, psychologically, mentally, materially, financially, and relationally alive and whole. We are to be agents of healing and wholeness to our spouses, as well.

Michael's wife Jane was a chain smoker – at one time, up to more than three packs a day. Both Michael and Jane were believers in Christ, and Michael had a growing conviction that he and Jane should become agents of healing to each other. A casual smoker himself, Michael took the initial step of putting an end to his own cigarette smoking. He then began to pray that Jane would have both the desire and the ability to quit smoking.

At first, Jane resisted Michael's suggestion that she stop smoking. Over time, Jane decided she too would give up cigarettes mostly due to Michael's encouragement presented in positive, noncritical ways. She found the challenge nearly overwhelming, however.

Michael continued to pray for her and with her that she would be able to live a cigarette-free life. He also sought out the prayers of others on Jane's behalf. It was in a prayer meeting with a few close friends that deliverance finally came for Jane. She immediately was freed from all craving for cigarettes and she has lived a cigarette-free life for several years now.

Michael brought about greater wholeness to Jane and truly was an agent of healing in her life. In turn, of course, Michael and Jane found that they had a stronger marriage relationship. Jane appreciated the fact that Michael had been patient with her and had desired her best. Michael was blessed in having a wife who suddenly had more energy, more enthusiasm for living, and a much greater degree of health.

Georgianna's story is much different, although her motivation was the same as Michael's.

After several years of marriage, Georgianna recognized in her husband a very deep hurt and need for love. She wisely discerned that this need was rooted in her husband having grown up in a home that was long on criticism and judgment and short on affection and praise. In their courtship, Georgianna had thought that her husband Frank's low self-esteem was something that would disappear once they were married, but it had not. Georgianna determined within herself to become an agent of healing and wholeness for her husband.

First, Georgianna made a commitment to pray daily for her husband. Each week she prayed for something very specific as a "theme" for her prayers. One week, for example, she prayed that he would be healed in his memories of all those times in which his father had criticized him publicly. Another week, she prayed that he would be able to accept her words of praise as being genuine and important. And so forth. Georgianna was very precise in her prayers and in focusing her faith.

Second, she made a commitment to speak as many words of genuine praise as she could to her husband. She acknowledged with thanksgiving every act of kindness; she praised every accomplishment; she pointed out with gratitude the many fine qualities which her husband displayed to her. Again, she was very specific and detailed. She once found herself saying, "Frank, I'm really glad you aren't like some men who seem to move from one channel on the remote control to the next, so that their wives never can watch more than fifteen seconds of a program at any one time." It was a strange compliment, but she meant what she said.
Indeed, in all of her compliments, Georgianna made sure she was genuine and that she truly meant what she said.

Third, Georgianna asked Frank if they might read the Scriptures and pray together on a daily basis — for just five minutes. After breakfast each morning, Georgianna would hand Frank the family Bible and he would read aloud from it for three or four minutes. Then, they would pray together. Georgianna often prayed for Frank that he would be blessed during the coming day to have people appreciate him and value him as much as she did. As often as possible, she would say at some point during the day how grateful she was for a Christian husband who was so loved by God.

Over time, Frank blossomed. He began to see himself as having great value in Georgianna's eyes, and also to see himself as a beloved child of God.

Did this impact their marriage? Of course. The more Frank came to value and appreciate himself, the easier it was for him to compliment Georgianna and show her how much he valued and appreciated her. In Georgianna's words, their marriage became a "mutual admiration society."

Frank became a more whole person as the result of what Georgianna did for him out of her selfless giving, generous prayers, and loving statements. Their marriage also became more whole.

As God is our Jehovah-Rophe, may we also be "healers" to others at every opportunity and in every area of life.

Jehovah-Nissi: Our Banner

When the children of Israel entered the Wilderness of Sin after their release from Egypt, they were attacked by the Amalekites. The children of Israel were not equipped for war and had no experience as warriors. For hundreds of years, they had been slaves in Egypt, the epitome of controlled passivity, not aggressive conquest. Here is what God told His people to do —

> *Moses instructed Joshua to issue a call to arms to the Israelites, to fight the army of Amalek. "Tomorrow," Moses told him, "I will stand at the top of the hill, with the rod of God in my hand!"*

So Joshua and his men went out to fight the army of Amalek. Meanwhile Moses, Aaron, and Hur went to the top of the hill.

And as long as Moses held up the rod in his hands, Israel was winning; but whenever he rested his arms at his sides, the soldiers of Amalek were winning.

Moses' arms finally became too tired to hold up the rod any longer; so Aaron and Hur rolled a stone for him to sit on, and they stood on each side, holding up his hands until sunset.

As a result, Joshua and his troops crushed the army of Amalek, putting them to the sword. . . .

Moses built an altar there and called it "Jehovah-nissi"

Exodus 17:9–13,15 (TLB)

Jehovah-Nissi literally means "Jehovah is my flag" or "Jehovah is my banner."

For thousands of years, armies have been identified by their banners. Banners are used to depict the origin and loyalty of a people, and especially an army. Moses was leading a people whose banner was the name of God. He was with them as they entered any conflict or any new territory.

Tough battles are a part of life for all of us. If you haven't just come out of a tough battle, you are likely going through one or you are about to face one. We live in a world where Satan is unrelentless in his pursuit of God's people and in his desire to see God's people fall into sin.

Throughout the Scriptures, we find repeated promises of God that He will be with us, and that He will help us overcome the enemy and endure all manners of persecution. One of the Lord's great promises is, "I will never leave thee, nor forsake thee" (Hebrews 13:5.) Paul was quick to write about God to the Romans: "If God be for us, who can be against us?" (Romans 8:31.) We are under God's banner and therefore, His presence is with us always and thus, our victory is ensured.

How can we function in God's likeness as Jehovah-Nissi to those around us?

• **Lifting Up Jesus.** We are always to be a person who raises high the banner of God. We can lift up Jesus in every circumstance, exalting Him as the answer to life's problems and the source of all that is good. We lift Him up every time we declare Him to be sovereign, the Savior, and the victor over evil. We are to point others to the truth that God is our shield, our defender, and our deliverer.

When Joel and Marta hit a tough circumstance in their marriage – the loss of Joel's job and simultaneously, Marta's diagnosis with breast cancer – they realized they each had a role to encourage the other to believe that God would bring them through this difficult time. Joel began to pray daily for Marta's health. Marta began to pray daily that Joel would find a good and fulfilling job.

They did not stop with prayer. Marta did her best to encourage Joel – reminding him of all God's promises to provide for him and sharing with him her own enthusiasm that he was a man with many talents and skills. Each day, she sent him out to search for a job with a positive outlook that God would provide and that Joel had many talents to offer a potential employer.

For his part, Joel reminded Marta of God's many promises to heal her body. He made a concerted effort to be with her when she had certain medical tests and treatments. He helped her when she suffered from the side effects of chemotherapy and he was her number-one nurse at the time she had surgery for removal of the malignant tumor. He was her foremost cheerleader during her recovery and as she regained her health.

At all times, Joel and Marta looked to God as the One whom they were following and the One who would win the battle on their behalf. They reminded each other on a daily basis that God was Jehovah-Nissi – He was leading the way into the battle and the victory was ensured.

Not only can we each be a person who raises high the banner of God and the name of Jesus to our spouse and others, but we can be a strong ally in times of spiritual warfare.

• **An Ally in Spiritual Warfare.** A second way we can mirror the nature of Jehovah Nissi to others is to fight alongside them as they wage spiritual warfare against the enemy of their lives.

Be your husband's foremost ally as he faces the daily battles of life. Be your wife's strong support as she faces the difficulties of each day. Be the one who says, "You can do this in Christ, for you can do all things through Christ who strengthens you." (See Philippians 4:13.)

Pray with your spouse against the enemy of your souls and your marriage. Stand strong against the outside forces that seek to destroy your witness, your reputation, your marriage, your health, your spiritual growth, your career progress, your finances, your emotional well-being. Become a united front.

A woman once noted that when she and her brother were children, they never even thought about asking their parents for certain things (which they knew were on the fringe of being harmful or wrong) because they knew their parents would provide a unified opinion. They never could pit one parent against the other. Whatever one said, the other parent backed up. "We didn't get away with nuthin'!" she said. "And I'm so glad now that we didn't."

Be so solid in your support of your spouse that it would be evident to any one who tried to attack one of you, that in attacking you, they were really attacking both of you. Fight for the honor and reputation of your spouse. Fight for the integrity of your marriage. Fight for the unity and the spiritual wholeness of your family. And always, fight under the banner of Jehovah-Nissi.

Just as God is the "sovereign" in whose kingdom we dwell, so we are to become kings and queens – together, as a single functioning monarchy – over the homes that we govern. Jesus is our number-one ally and identity; our spouse is our number-two ally and point of identification!

Jehovah-Mekaddish: The Holy One Who Makes Holy

When God gave His people the design for their worship life, He also gave them a very specific design for the tabernacle, the vessels in it, and the priests who were to function as part of that worship life. The laws that were given regarding this were simple but very specific. They became the foundation for the justice system that we have throughout the Western world.

In Exodus 31:12–13,16,17 (TLB) we read about a very special description that God associates with His name –

The Lord then gave these further instructions to Moses:

"Tell the people of Israel to rest on my Sabbath day, for the Sabbath is a reminder of the covenant between me

> *and you forever; it helps you to remember that I am Jehovah who makes you holy....*
>
> *Work six days only, for the seventh day is a special day of solemn rest, holy to the Lord....*
>
> *It is an eternal symbol of the covenant between me and the people of Israel. For in six days the Lord made heaven and earth, and rested on the seventh day, and was refreshed.*

Jehovah-Mekaddish literally means "The God Who Makes Holy." How does God make us holy, which means separated unto Himself and away from all the world? There are two great signs or marks of holiness which God prescribed for His people: circumcision for all males, and the keeping of the Sabbath by both men and women. These two outward signs were a great witness to the rest of the world, which did not adhere to circumcision and which did not keep a day of rest from labor. These were the marks that "separated" the children of Israel from all other peoples in an outward and visible way.

The Sabbath was clearly intended to be a reminder of the covenant. God wanted His people to remember and to renew their covenant vow with Him on a weekly basis. He knew that if they ever forgot the living reality of their covenant with Him, they would be setting themselves up for disaster.

Sacrifices reminded the people of their sin and their need for forgiveness, but it was the Sabbath, primarily, that reminded the people that God is holy. He is above, He is separate, His ways are higher than man's ways, He is absolute perfection and purity.

The Sabbath was also a time for remembering that God had called His people to be like Him in these ways — to operate according to a different set of commandments and schedule than the rest of the world, to be pure and perfect in ways that the world was not pure or perfect, and to be totally dependent upon God in a way that other peoples were not.

None of us is holy in and of ourselves. Any holiness that we might bear is a gift of God through Jesus Christ. He is our holiness. But what we can each do for one another is to encourage those around us to be holy – to be separated unto God and to be separated from a sinful world.

In a marriage relationship, we can encourage holiness in our spouses in the following ways:

• **Keep the Sabbath.** We mirror the nature of Jehovah-Mekaddish when we keep the Sabbath. We must set aside the Sabbath as a time of rest and family worship of God. The old saying, "The family that prays together is a family that stays together" has merit, but the saying might very well be adapted to convey an even greater truth: "The family that keeps the Sabbath together is a family that finds holiness together."

The Sabbath is to be more than a day of attending church services. It is a day designed to provide "refreshment" for a person – to provide rest, recreation, and nourishment for the soul and spirit. Make the Sabbath a day in which you not only go to church together but that you find an opportunity to relax together, play together, talk together, sing together, and to enjoy one another's company.

As you are together on the Sabbath, include in your conversation an acknowledgment of the many blessings that God has provided for you during the past week. Praise and offer thanks to God for the good things that He has done for you, in you, and through you. Consider these dozen things which the Lord does for us on an ongoing basis, although we rarely stop to thank Him for doing them:

• Keeps us healthy and safe — or helping us to overcome a sickness or injury
• Provides sufficient and nutritious food for us to eat
• Provides friends for us
• Helps us to do the work He has put before us to do — including schoolwork and housework
• Gives us keen minds that are able to learn new things every day
• Watches over us as we sleep so that no harm comes to us in the night — including guarding our dreams
• Gives us new ideas and inspirations about things we might do in the coming days
• Helps us to communicate and to express ourselves
• Shows us creative ways to solve problems and settle disputes
• Provides for us sufficient water to drink, clean air to breathe, adequate clothing to wear, and protective shelter
• Gives us such a beautiful world in which to live
• Gives us the gift of family

Be mindful of the many ways in which God has been present with you. Voice your praise that God has helped you even when you were unaware of His help!

• **Support Your Spouse in a Holy Life.** A second way in which we can mirror the identity of Jehovah-Mekaddish is to support our spouse's efforts to live a holy life. A holy life is characterized by dedication and consecration to God and a life that seeks to be separated from the evil and sin of the world.

Never make fun of your spouse for being "too good." Rather, support your spouse's efforts to be more like Christ. Don't criticize your spouse for failing to participate in the sin of your choice — to the contrary, applaud your spouse for standing strong in faith and for having a desire to pursue all things that are righteous and pure.

Praise your spouse for the choices that your spouse makes to disengage from sinful activities and to drop sinful associations. Go with your spouse to church and to church-related meetings, concerts, retreats, and special events. Be supportive of your spouse's need to carve out time in each day to be alone with the Lord, to pray, and to read and study the Bible.

The more you encourage your husband or wife to a life of holiness, the more you will find an atmosphere of "rest" settling over your family and home.

Many married couples complain, "We never have enough time together" or "My spouse doesn't spend enough time with me." Keeping a Sabbath day together and accompanying your spouse to events and activities in which the Lord is exalted is a prime way to spend time together. In renewing your covenant relationship with God, you will also be renewing your covenant relationship with each other.

• **Remind Your Spouse of Your Covenant Relationship.** A third way to help your spouse walk in holiness is to provide gentle reminders to your spouse of your covenant relationship in marriage and how valuable you consider this covenant relationship to be. One of the best and easiest ways to do this is to continue to date, no matter how long you have been married. Find ways to spend an evening alone together, or a weekend together now and then.

Never let a day go by without telling your spouse, "I love you." Call your spouse by what he or she is to you – saying, "I love you, my husband" or "I love you, my wife." Let your spouse know that you are grateful to be in your marriage relationship.

One man made it a habit to tell his wife each day, "I am so glad that I am your husband. I am the luckiest man alive." She, in turn, said the same thing back to him, "And I'm so glad I'm your wife. I'm the luckiest woman alive." Together, of course, they were two of the luckiest people on earth!

From time to time, do things that will especially enrich your marriage. You may want to go on a marriage-enrichment retreat together, or take a special trip together or perhaps go with another couple or two who are close friends and who have strong marriages.

And finally, make it a point always to speak well of marriage to others. This goes beyond praising or acknowledging the good traits of your spouse. Be grateful for your marriage. Although you might admit that you both have flaws and therefore your marriage has problems – which is a reality for all couples – speak well of the fact that you are married and that you choose to remain married.

Lift up the institution of marriage as something to be valued in our culture, and something which you value in your personal life. Avoid saying such things as, "If only I wasn't married" or "I might be better off not married." Be grateful for your marriage and affirm your commitment to stay in your marriage.

Jehovah-Shalom: Our Peace

In Gideon's day, Israel was little more than a group of downtrodden people who were put down by every passing king, thug, and thief. Gideon himself was hiding from the invading Midianites when an angel of the Lord said to him, "Mighty soldier, the Lord is with you!" (Judges 6:12 TLB). Gideon felt like anything but a mighty soldier at that moment. He was hiding in a wine vat! He responded –

> *"Stranger . . . if the Lord is with us, why has all this happened to us? And where are all the miracles our ances-*

tors have told us about – such as when God brought them out of Egypt? Now the Lord has thrown us away and has let the Midianites completely ruin us."

Then the Lord turned to him and said, "I will make you strong! Go and save Israel from the Midianites! I am sending you!"

Judges 6:13-14 (TLB)

Gideon responded to this statement from the angel by making a sacrifice to God, which the angel struck with fire. Gideon was in awe at what had happened, and also very fearful that he might die for having seen and talked with an angel. The Lord spoke to him, "Peace be unto thee; fear not: thou shalt not die (Judges 6:23). In response, Gideon built an altar and named it "Jehovah-Shalom."

Jehovah-Shalom literally means "God of Peace." An even fuller definition might be, "God of Peace with God." The peace which is referenced here is not the "absence of war" or the "absence of fighting." It is a genuine peace that is born of faith and trust in God regardless of outer circumstances. In other words, it is having inner spiritual peace even in the presence of war or conflict!

Gideon was experiencing this peace even though he was still in a land occupied and ruled by Midianites. He had this peace even though all of his outer circumstances seemed to be ones that spelled oppression, depression, and repression.

Again and again throughout the Bible we find God saying to His people, "Fear not." These were the words of Jesus when He appeared to them behind closed doors after His resurrection. Our automatic response is to be frightened at God's awesome presence with us. His response to us is, "Peace."

Once we have fully experienced God's peace in our hearts, we have a confidence that we can and will come through any situation victoriously. Even if we die, the apostles taught, we die in Christ and are with Him forever! Nothing can separate us from the love of God, and therefore, nothing can strip away from us the inner peace which God's prevailing and loving presence creates in us.

As the recipients of God's peace, we are also to become agents of God's peace. We are to be peacemakers – bringing others to full reconciliation with God, and with each other. "Blessed are the peacemakers," Jesus taught, "for they shall be called the children of God." (See Matthew 5:9.)

How, specifically, might we reflect God's "Jehovah-Shalom" nature to our spouses and other family members?

First and foremost, we can speak words of peace whenever conflict or arguments arise, which they inevitably do in any relationship. This does not mean, of course, that we "roll over and play dead" any time a conflict arises, or that we allow others to manipulate us or run over us in an abusive way. Rather, it means that when difficulties arise, we can do these very specific things:

• **Speak in a Tone of Peace.** We each can govern our speech so that we speak with a tone of peace. We do not need to elevate our voices or to express our anger in either verbal or nonverbal ways. We can establish within ourselves a demeanor and a tone of peace.

• **Listen Fully.** We each have the ability to listen fully to the other person in an attitude of peace until the other person has fully expressed himself or herself. Very often just listening to another person fully and without interruption brings about a more peaceful atmosphere in which a reasonable conversation or discussion can occur.

• **Pray for Peace.** We have it within our ability to turn to God and ask Him to give us His peace. Even if your spouse does not desire God's peace, your desire for God's peace should not be diminished. Ask God to reveal to you the way He would have you deal with the conflict, argument, or difference of opinion. Be open to areas in which your own pride and self-centeredness may be clouding your vision about an appropriate course of action. If you are feeling wounded, rejected, hurt, or angry at what another person has done or said, ask God to heal you of that emotion and to help you respond in a way that is loving and kind.

Ultimately, only the Lord can bring peace to our hearts. You cannot force another person to a position of peace, and neither can another person "heal" your deep inner wounds. Only God can truly help you feel accepted, valued, and loved. Only God can take away the sting of anger or remove a root of bitterness from your soul. Only God can replace the hate in a heart with genuine love and concern.

• **Choose NOT to Fuel the Argument.** We are wise not to add "fuel to the fire" of another person's anger or hatred. The wrong time to talk to a person who is extremely upset is while they are upset! Wait until things calm down before you express your opinion or desires. Make certain that what you are going to say to the other person is firmly rooted in love and that it is not intended to provoke, retaliate, or exact revenge. Many a conflict can be defused if a person simply does not respond immediately to the anger or bitterness that is spewed out by another person.

One of the things that often occurs during times of conflict is *confusion.* A person may feel blindsided by an argument or blast of anger and not know immediately what to say or how to respond. In confusion, the person begins to feel hurt and alienated. In those cases, give yourself some time to digest exactly what the person was saying and perhaps to discern why. If you are unsure about how to respond, go to God's Word. Ask God to reveal to you the appropriate way you *should* feel and how you should respond.

In being a reflection of our God of Peace – Jehovah-Shalom – we are to be agents of peace in our families, churches, work places, and communities. First, however, we must become bearers of God's peace within our own hearts and minds.

Jehovah-Tsidkenu: Our Righteousness

The prophet Jeremiah lived in a day when the Israelites had completely lost their way in a heathen world. Wicked kings led the people into bowing to false gods. Rebellion was rampant. Jeremiah was a voice of warning, and also a voice of the "reality" of God's chastisement of His people. He also foresaw a day, however, when God would reveal a plan for redemption from their failures and sins. In Jeremiah 23:5-6 we have these words of the prophet –

> *Behold, the days come, saith the Lord, that I will raise unto David a righteous Branch, and a King shall reign and prosper, and shall execute judgment and justice in the earth.*
>
> *In his days Judah shall be saved, and Israel shall dwell safely: and this is his name whereby he shall be called, THE LORD OUR RIGHTEOUSNESS.*

This description of God as "The Lord Our Righteousness" points out to us that the God who is in covenant with us is not only a God of great mercy and fathomless love, but a God who demands justice, righteousness, and purity. Sin has no part in God and therefore, God will always remove sin from Himself. That is the basis on which sin is "punished" – it simply is removed far from God, and to be away from God's abiding presence and power is, to be certain, the worst punishment mankind can ever experience. To be in close relationship with God is life and blessing. To be removed from God's presence is to experience death and unpleasant consequences.

All sin has consequences – some immediate, some delayed. This is God's truth from the beginning. And also from the beginning, the only means of removing the consequences of sin from a person's life has been a blood sacrifice. The reason for this is very simple: life and the flow of blood are intricately and inseparably intertwined. Life does not exist without the flow of blood; blood does not flow without life. A sacrifice involving blood speaks to the fact that man cannot experience life and blessing apart from God.

God was the first to initiate a blood sacrifice when He killed animals and used their skins to cover the nakedness of Adam and Eve. In doing this, God was giving Adam and Eve an ever-present reminder that the only means they had for life and blessing was to be in obedient relationship to Him.

The blood sacrifices which God commanded the children of Israel to make were for the same reason – to be an ever-present reminder that God is the Source of Life. Ultimately, the death of Jesus Christ on the cross, as the one true and lasting sacrifice for sin, was a blood sacrifice. In Christ's death lies our life!

The death of Jesus calls us into relationship with God and is the provision for that relationship to exist. The very name of Jesus means "Jehovah Is Salvation." (See Matthew 1:25.) Jesus is our means of salvation. He is Savior.

The only way a person can live in a righteous state before God is to appropriate – or to claim as one's own – the sacrifice of Jesus on the cross. To do so is to say, "Jesus died for me. He is my Savior."

Apart from the blood covenant, we cannot experience righteousness. Righteousness is not a matter of "keeping the rules," or doing the right thing, or being a "good person" as many believe. Righteousness is experienced only through having a relationship with Jesus Christ. The righteousness we have is actually His righteousness, freely extended to us because of our belief in Him. Righteousness is never something we can achieve, earn, purchase, or acquire on our own strength.

Righteousness within a relationship is not nagging another person to keep God's commandments or to do what we perceive to be the "right" things. Righteousness is not insisting that a person obey certain laws or follow certain rituals. Rather, righteousness in a relationship is encouraging another person to have a close relationship with Jesus Christ.

An amazing thing happens when we draw closer to Christ — sins seem to slough away from us. The desire to disobey God disappears. A person wants to serve God, obey God, and do what is pleasing to the heart of God.

How might a person encourage a spouse to have a deeper relationship with Christ?

• **Don't Criticize Godly Activities.** Never criticize your spouse for wanting to spend time with the Lord. Don't be jealous of the time that your spouse spends in prayer or reading the Word. In fact, you are wise if you suggest from time to time that your spouse go on a spiritual retreat so that your spouse might renew his or her covenant relationship with God.

• **Participate with Your Spouse in Godly Activities.** Join your spouse in times of prayer, spiritual refreshment, and worship of the Lord. Pray together. Read the Bible together. Attend church social activities together. Work in ministry outreaches together. The more you serve and worship Christ together, the more righteousness will reign in both of your hearts and in your home.

• **Build Your Family Schedule Around the Lord.** Construct your family schedule and social activities around events that build relationship with the Lord. Consider going to a Christian campground or retreat center for a family vacation – a campground that offers activities for both children and adults of all ages. Attend Christian concerts and theatrical performances together as a family. Rent Christ-centered or Christ-honoring videos to watch as a family. Have a family prayer time every day – perhaps before you leave the house in the morning or before you go to bed.

Give priority to those events that are related to the church and to having a relationship with Christ. Don't let a soccer schedule keep you from church!

Encourage your children to belong to youth groups that are Christ-centered or which are related to your church.

Yvonne was convicted on this point of encouraging her husband in righteousness and encouraging him to have a deeper relationship with Christ. She had been very envious of the times that her husband went on fishing trips with men from their church. Rather than encouraging her husband to spend time with Christian men, she had wanted him to spend all of his "free" time with her. She was especially envious of the hours that her husband withdrew to his study to "be with God." She felt that he was withdrawing form her and the children more than he was withdrawing to be with the Lord.

In prayer one day, the Lord spoke to Yvonne's heart, "Don't keep your husband from My presence. If you do, how can I mold him into the man I want him to be?" Yvonne felt deeply moved and convicted. She asked the Lord to forgive her.

Yvonne began to encourage her husband to attend men's retreats and to be involved with the men of their church in various activities. In turn, her husband became much more encouraging of her desire to attend women's retreats. When her husband retreated to spend time with the Lord, she spent that time on chores and other activities that would not have involved her husband anyway. Best of all, the resentment she had felt in her heart melted away. Her husband's relationship with the Lord flourished, and as it did, of course, so did his relationship with Yvonne. Usually what keeps a husband or wife from desiring a spouse to have a deeper relationship with the Lord is a fear or a resentment that if the spouse spends more time with the Lord, he or she will spend less time with the family. That is rarely the case! If a person feels free to spend time with the Lord, he or she is likely to want to spend even more quality time with spouse and children.

Don't let your pride get in the way. Encourage relationship with God. That is the key to bringing righteousness into your home. As God is Our Righteousness, so we must do all we can to encourage righteousness in others – and that means that we encourage relationship with Christ Jesus!

Taking On God's Identity

God not only reveals to us His name, but He gives us His name. In the next chapter we will deal with two additional names that God has given to us, as well as the name of Jesus.

When we take a look at the whole of the names of Jesus, we see a wonderful identity that we are to have as Christians.
God is our provider, and we are to provide for others.
God is our healer, and we are to be agents of healing to others.
God is our banner, and we are to lift up the name of Christ Jesus to others so that they may follow Him and be blessed.
God is our means of holiness, and we are to live holy lives.
God is our peace, and we are to be ambassadors of peace.
God is our righteousness, and we are to live righteous lives.

Not only does God call us to assume His identity in our lives and marriages, but He empowers us to do so. He gives us His Spirit so that we might be the very people He calls us to be!

Take courage today in your marriage. God has a wonderful role for you to play in the life of your spouse and as a witness to God's great love.

Scriptures That Confirm:

God Gives Us His Identity So That We Might Do What He Would Do

If my people, which are called by my name, shall humble themselves, and pray, and seek my face, and turn from their wicked ways; then will I hear from heaven, and will forgive their sin, and will heal their land

2 Chronicles 7:14
(Underline added for emphasis.)

I will praise thee, O Lord, with my whole heart; I will shew forth all thy marvelous works.

I will be glad and rejoice in thee: I will sing praise to thy name, O thou most High

Psalm 9:1–2

Thy statutes have been my songs in the house of my pilgrimage.

I have remembered thy name, O Lord, in the night, and have kept thy law

Psalm 119:54–55

Be ye therefore perfect, even as your Father which is in heaven is perfect

Matthew 5:48

Jesus said unto them, Come ye after me, and I will make you to become fishers of men

Mark 1:17

[Jesus said], Father, glorify thy name. Then came there a void from heaven, saying, I have both glorified it, and will glorify it again

John 12:28

Epaphras, who is one of you, a servant of Christ, saluteth you, always laboring fervently for you in prayers, that ye may stand perfect and complete in all the will of God

Colossians 4:12

Chapter 6

Chapter 6

God Gives Us His Name as Our Indentity (Part 2)

God, especially as He revealed Himself in the Old Testament, was an "awesome," and unapproachable God. The Israelites were in fearful reverence of Him at all times. They believed that to hear God's voice was a stunning occurrence, and to see God meant death. The fact that the Almighty had extended His name to His people, revealed His character to them and called them to not only adopt but abide in His character, was a wonderful and holy gift.

We are wise always to take seriously the fact that God has not only revealed Himself to us through Jesus Christ, but that He calls us to be like Jesus. Perhaps the most precious and certainly the most potent force on this earth is the name of God – Father, Son, and Holy Spirit. In His name is life-changing power.

In the previous chapter we dealt with six facets of God's name as revealed through the adjectives linked to the name Jehovah. In this chapter, we will cover two additional names that speak to us of God's identity, and therefore, our call and challenge as we seek to be more and more like our Heavenly Father's begotten Son, Jesus Christ.

Jehovah-Shammah: Ever-Present God

The prophet Ezekiel had a vision of the future where Israel would be led into captivity, Jerusalem and the Temple destroyed, and the land devastated. He also foresaw, however, the time when God would do something "bigger and better" – the tribes would be reestablished and live in peace, Jerusalem would be rebuilt, and God's presence would be restored in a magnificent Temple. The very last verse of Ezekiel (48:35) gives us another descriptor for God that is associated with that time –

> *The name of the city from that day shall be, The Lord is there.*

Jehovah-Shammah literally means "God Is Present." Throughout the Scriptures, we find many references to God's eternal, abiding, and ever-present nature. He said to Moses, "I AM WHO I AM." God was and will be, but ultimately, God is. He does not change, which means that in every moment of every hour of every day of every year of every century of every millennium God is just the same in character and nature. Therefore, He can always be trusted because He is always present and He is always the same.

Mankind has experienced this presence of God in different ways. In Old Testament times, only the high priest who entered the Holy of Holies on one day a year came into the direct presence of God. That encounter with the living God was so awesome and of such great importance that a rope was tied to the high priest's ankle so that if his life appeared to be unfit to God and he died as a result, his body could be pulled back out of the Holy of Holies.

The covenant established by Jesus Christ made God's presence much more accessible. As the writer of Hebrews says, we now can "come boldly before the throne of grace." (See Hebrews 4:16.) God no longer resides in a building or a temple. Rather, He resides within His people. His Holy Spirit is freely poured out upon all who will believe and accept the blood sacrifice of Jesus Christ on the cross.

The presence of God is experienced in a special way when

"two or three are gathered" in the name of Jesus. He says, "there am I in the midst of you." (See Matthew 18:20.)

Through the covenant made with Jesus Christ, God has revealed Himself as the self-existent God who is always with us, closer than the very breath we breathe. Nothing can separate us or divide us from access to Him. He is with us *always*. As Jesus says in Revelation 22:13, "I am Alpha and Omega, the beginning and the end, the first and the last." His promise to us is, "Lo, I am with you alway, even unto the end of the world" (Matthew 28:20).

None of us can be ever-present for another person. We are creatures of change, growth, development, and also creatures who are bound to a natural order that includes death. How then might we reflect the covenant name of Jehovah-Shammah to others around us, and especially to a spouse? We can do this in three very practical ways.

• **Stay in Your Marriage.** Make it very clear to your spouse that you are not leaving your marriage. Dora Griego made that very clear to Ron Griego when he proposed marriage to her. She said, "Make sure this is what you want because I will never give you a divorce."

Never tease about divorce or threaten divorce to your spouse. Some people use the threat of divorce as a means of manipulating a spouse to get what they want. That's dangerous ground to tread.

Assure your spouse that you will be there for him or her and that you are faithful to your marriage vows. Then give your spouse no cause for suspicion. Be there when your spouse needs you.

• **Be Consistent.** Strive to be consistent in yourself and in your relationship with your spouse. Roller coasters may be fun to ride in an amusement park setting, but nobody enjoys living with a person who has roller-coaster emotions — up one day, down the next, continually shifting positions, opinions, and beliefs. Values are to be rock-solid, not floating with the circumstances. Beliefs are to be consistent, not changing with the tides.

Sam never knew who was going to be behind the door of his home when he went home at night. Oh, he knew it would be his wife Trina, but he never knew "which Trina" might greet him. Would it be the angry Trina, the pouting Trina, the cool-calm-and-collected Trina, the fun-loving Trina, or the ready-for-a-fight Trina? Although Trina was a believer in Jesus Christ, she also was, in her pastor's terms, "wound up very tight."

The result of Trina's wide mood swings, quite naturally, was that Sam began to dread going home. He started the bad habit of stopping for a drink or two before going home, in his words, to "bolster myself" for whatever he might face. Eventually, Sam started spending more and more time away from the house – which made Trina all the more erratic and volatile in her emotions.

It was through good Christian pastoral counseling that Trina began to see the great damage she was doing to her marriage. She was being far from a reflection of her Lord, Jehovah-Shammah, in her relationship with Sam. She confessed her failure to the Lord and asked for His help.

One of the things that came out of this particular situation was the fact that Trina suffered from a chemical imbalance. She received a healing in her body through medications. She also made a concerted effort to be more consistent in her emotions, and especially in those she displayed in Sam's presence. If she felt angry or upset, she went to the Lord with those emotions and poured her heart out to God before Sam came home. Rather than dump her anxieties, fears, and hurts upon Sam, she laid them on the altar of her heart before God.

Sam, of course, began to find more and more reasons to come

straight home to Trina. No more stopping at the local bar. No more finding excuses to stay at work late or to run extra errands. Trina, in return, was delighted that Sam was spending more time with her and that their times together were more enjoyable for both of them.

• **Be "Present" and Available.** Support your spouse with your presence. This does not mean that you need to be with your spouse twenty-four hours a day. It does mean that there are times and ways in which you can be present for your spouse as a source of encouragement and strength.

If your spouse has an important event or party to attend, go with him (if that is appropriate). Be *with* him while you are there – rather than abandoning him to go in search of your friends. Attend award ceremonies or other times of recognition for your husband.

A man once was asked how he knew his wife was faithful and loyal to him. He replied, "She attends all of my softball games."

On the surface, this reply may have been seen to be a statement equal to, "I know she isn't cheating on me because I know where she's at – she's at my games." On a deeper level, however, this man was stating the truth, "My wife is loyal to me even to the degree that she supports me in what is important to me."

Now, this wife didn't particularly like the game of softball, but she went to the games in support of her husband. The games were important to him, and therefore, she made them an important part of her schedule. She took along a bag of knitting, which was an enjoyable pastime for her, and she developed friendships with some of the other wives. Her support of her husband's hobby was a clear sign to her husband of her faithfulness and her "ever-presence" for him.

We have all heard children bemoan the fact that their parents weren't present for their school play or their big game or their award ceremony. The same hurt feelings often exist for a spouse! Be there when your spouse needs your supportive presence.

As another example, Tim supports DeeDee with his presence by coming home on Monday nights by seven o'clock so that DeeDee can attend a Bible study that she values greatly. Monday is Tim's night to be responsible for the children. DeeDee sees this as a great gift of love to her. In effect, Tim is "present" for DeeDee by being present with their children.

You can never be *omnipresent* (always present). But you can be consistently and willingly present. You can choose to be present when it matters most to your spouse.

Jehovah-Rohi: The Great Shepherd

Perhaps one of the most often quoted and best known verses in the entire Bible is a verse that reveals yet another facet of God's covenant nature. Psalm 23:1 says, "The Lord is my shepherd; I shall not want."

Jehovah-Rohi literally means, "The Lord Is Shepherd." This image of God as the Great Shepherd is one that is present throughout the Bible. The concept is that

- God takes care of us, just as a shepherd tends his flocks.
- God leads us, just as a shepherd leads his flocks to green pastures and good sources of water.
- God defends us, just as a shepherd fends off lions, bears, and other wild animals in defense of his flocks.
- God looks out for us, saving us from our own craziness and weakness and keeps us from "wandering away" or "falling off ledges." Even the weakest and youngest of sheep is important to a shepherd. And so are we to God.

Jesus identified with this image of a good and loving shepherd. He said —

> *I am the good shepherd: the good shepherd giveth his life for the sheep.*
>
> *But he that is an hireling, and not the shepherd, whose own the sheep are not, seeth the wolf coming, and leaveth the sheep, and fleeth: and the wolf catcheth them, and scattereth the sheep.*
>
> *The hireling fleeth, because he is an hireling, and careth not for the sheep.*
>
> *I am the good shepherd, and know my sheep, and am known of mine.*
>
> *As the Father knoweth me, even so know I the Father: and I lay down my life for the sheep*
>
> John 10:11–15

What comfort we can take in knowing that the Lord is our Good Shepherd! Like sheep, we often do things that are foolish and destructive to ourselves. Yet the Lord takes care of us and rescues us from ourselves. He watches our every move.

How might we be more like Jehovah-Rohi to others?

· **Seek to Be Helpful.** First, we are always to look for ways in which we might be of help to others. This does not mean that we are to smother others with our constant presence or care, or that we are to do things for others that they can or should do for themselves. Rather, it means that we have a heart of genuine care and concern for the well-being of others — yes, even a care and concern equal to what we have for ourselves.

In Christ, there is no "looking out for number-one." We are to look out for both ourselves and others with an equal passion. We each are called to be self-giving and generous toward others, especially those in need.

Our help is never to be that which enables a person to sin or to continue in a bad habit. Rather, it is to be genuine help that encourages a person to draw closer to Christ and to exhibit more of Christ's character and strength in his or her life.

Being of help does not mean that we are to nag or chide others, but that we are to lift up others and call them to have an even greater and more noble vision of themselves in Christ Jesus. Believing for the best in others leads us to help others become their best.

· **Be a Source of Moral Courage.** We are to be a source of strength and moral leadership in times when others are weak or confused. Every person has times when he or she is "down" – perhaps overly tired, a little confused on a particular issue, or in doubt. At times like this we must be strong – leading that person back to the Word of God to draw upon the rich nourishment of God's truth and promises. We must pray with the person, and encourage them to trust God's faithfulness and to rely upon the daily guidance and strength offered by the Holy Spirit.

Marie's friend Wanda was in the same boat as she – both had husbands who did not know Christ. They met twice a week for lunch and prayer. Actually, rather than eat lunch, they fasted through the noon hour as they prayed for their husbands. Since they were coworkers in the same company and at the same site, they simply went to a quiet corner of their building to spend the lunch period together. Their prayers were very specific and certainly heartfelt.

As would be expected, there were times when Marie would be

discouraged that she saw no signs of her husband having a growing interest in Christ. It was at those times that Wanda refused to "agree" with Marie or to wallow in her discouragement with her. Rather, she did what she could to build up Marie's faith and to encourage her to trust God to be faithful to His Word. At other times, it was Wanda who would become disheartened at the lack of progress she saw in her husband. Marie became her source of encouragement.

Together, the two women stayed true to their faith, loyal to their husbands, and in the end, both women saw their husbands come to Christ and become filled with God's Spirit. This result didn't happen overnight – it took three years for Marie's husband to come to Christ and nearly four years before Wanda's husband made a commitment of his life to the Lord. Even so, these women remained faithful friends to each other. After their husbands became Christians, they did not stop their lunch hour prayer meetings. They simply took on other prayer requests!

• **Intercede for Others.** Defend those you love in prayer – fighting spiritual battles on their behalf. The Good Shepherd fights for His flocks, and in the spiritual realm, we are to engage in battle for our spouses and children, as well as for other beloved family members and Christian brothers and sisters.

The weapons of our warfare are not carnal, or manmade. They are spiritual. We fight these battles in prayer – fully armed with the fullness of Christ's presence (His faith, His righteousness, His Gospel, His Truth) and with the Word of God. We speak the promises and provisions of God to the enemy. We declare God as victor. We pray in the powerful name of Jesus and we remind ourselves and the enemy of our souls that we are in covenant relationship with the Most High God.

One of the most important things that you can ever do for a spouse is to engage in intercessory prayer, especially when he or she is facing an intense time of conflict or temptations.

To be like Jehovah-Rohi, the Great Shepherd, means that we are to be our brother's keeper to the best of our ability. We are to "keep" the treasure of our spouse's, child's, and friend's confidences, confessions, and dreams. We are to "keep" the welfare and well-being of those we love as a top priority. We are to "keep" evil from touching those we love.

To this end, we are to guard the entrance to our homes carefully in order to keep out any one or any thing that might lead your spouse or one of your children into doubt, sin, or impurity.

Hallowing the Name of God

At all times, we are in a position within the covenant to be fulfilling the opening lines of the prayer that Jesus taught His disciples to pray: "Our Father which art in heaven, hallowed be thy name" (Matthew 6:9).

We are to consider God's name to be holy and we must approach both God and the use of His name with awesome reverence. What a tremendous heritage we are given in the covenant as God reveals, and thus gives, His name to us:

- Jehovah-Jireh — God Our Provider
- Jehovah-Rophe — God Our Healer
- Jehovah-Nissi — God Our Banner
- Jehovah-Mekaddish — God Our Holiness
- Jehovah-Shalom — God Our Peace
- Jehovah-Tsidkenu — God Our Righteousness
- Jehovah-Shammah — God Is Present
- Jehovah-Rohi — God Our Good Shepherd

When God gives us His name in covenant relationship, He also intends for us to operate within the context of that name in all of our other relationships. He calls us to provide, heal, establish, witness, encourage, uphold, and benefit others – and especially our spouse with whom we are in covenant relationship.

Jesus said plainly, "Freely ye have received, freely give" (Matthew 10:8.) That is our great challenge! As we have received so freely and richly all of the wonders of God's presence, so we must share freely with others the presence of God that is within us.

Bearing the Name of Christ Jesus

Not only do we have the names of God revealed to us to help us better understand who we are in covenant relationship with our Creator, but we have also been given the name of Jesus Christ as our identity and as our strength. By knowing the names by which God revealed himself, we can better understand God's character and how we are to respond to others. We also come into a greater understanding of what it means to live and act as a Christian when we know more fully all that has been given to us in the name of our Lord.

Our first and foremost use of the name of Jesus is to baptize others. We are to witness in the name of Jesus and to make disciples of all nations in His name. Jesus said to His disciples just shortly before His ascension into heaven –

> *Go ye therefore and teach all nations, baptizing them in the name of the Father, and of the Son, and of the Holy Ghost:*
>
> *Teaching them to observe all things whatsoever I have commanded you . . .*
>
> *Matthew 28:19-20*

We must never lose sight that one of the most important reasons for us to have a good marriage on this earth is so that we might be a witness to God's saving, healing, and restoring power to others. Your marriage sends a message to those who observe it. Either you are loving Christ and in His love, loving one another, or you are not loving Christ and therefore, are attempting to love one another in your own strength – which is a surefire recipe for periodic failures and breakdowns.

No person is able to sustain a loving relationship through all manner of conflict and trouble without drawing upon the love of God. People may try, and some couples may even appear to succeed, but their love will always be incomplete and unfulfilling to a degree because it does not include the spiritual dimension of love made possible only by Christ. Without a love that flows from the inner spirit of one's being, love is incomplete. For a person to have a truly satisfying, fulfilling love relationship with another person, God must be included.

One of the best reasons to choose to stay married and to stand for one's marriage no matter how difficult the situation is so that you together might send a message to the world that you believe in a God who is faithful, who loves in spite of flaws, and who is steadfast regardless of circumstances.

Signs Associated with Christ's Name

The great commission of Jesus to His disciples has this added statement as it appears in Mark 16:17-18 –

And these signs shall follow them that believe; In my name shall they cast out devils; they shall speak with new tongues;

they shall take up serpents; and if they drink any deadly

thing, it shall not hurt them; they shall lay hands on the sick, and they shall recover.

These promises and signs which Jesus "gave" to His followers are for us today, just as much as they were for the first disciples. Jesus has given to those who faithfully believe in Him many supernatural powers. This same principle extends to our relationships with others. All of the things that Jesus described in this passage are for the good of those who follow Christ. They are gifts that pertain to a person's spiritual health and wholeness, as well as to one's physical health and wholeness and to one's ability to help others.

When we enter into a covenant relationship with Christ and with a spouse who is a believer, we are given a great "gift" from Christ – His presence in our marriage. He promises to be with us every step of the way to make us spiritually, emotionally, and physically healthy and whole as marriage partners. He also will be with us to bring us into a ministry – together as a couple – that will help others and thus, will magnify and glorify His name.

Many scientific and medical studies have come out in recent years pointing to the "health benefits" that a good marriage affords – both physically and emotionally. Spiritually, marriage partners are to support one another so that together, the home they establish is spiritually sound. God's Word is true and we can count on it. God intends for us to live in wholeness, with a supernatural covering over our homes, as we are faithful in our covenant to Him and to each other.

• **Total Healing.** In Acts we read about an instance in which Peter and John ministered to a lame man at the Beautiful Gate to the Temple. This man had been trapped for years in a "broken body." We read –

Then Peter said, Silver and gold have I none; but such as I have give I thee: In the name of Jesus Christ of Nazareth rise up and walk.

And he took him by the right hand, and lifted him up: and immediately his feet and ankle bones received strength.

And he leaping up stood, and walked, and entered with them into the temple, walking, and leaping, and praising God

Acts 3:6–8

In another story of healing, we find that as Paul traveled in ministry, a young woman who was demon possessed hounded and brought ridicule to his work. We read –

But Paul, being grieved, turned and said to the spirit, I command thee in the name of Jesus Christ to come out of her. And he came out the same hour

Acts 16:18

What do these stories have to do with us today?

These stories teach us by example that the power of the name of Jesus provides for both physical healing and spiritual deliverance.

When we pray for one another – husbands and wives praying together, parents and children praying together – we can appropriate the name of Jesus for both physical and spiritual healing for our families. How important it is that we pray for one another *in the name of Jesus!* When your spouse or your children are sick, pray for them in His name! When your spouse or your children struggle with temptations, must face or confront persons with evil intent, or have nightmares that seem to torment . . . pray for them in Jesus' name! Send the spirits of sickness, torment, bondage, and oppression fleeing from your home!

Satan cannot stand against the name of Jesus. He must flee those who resist him in Christ's name. Paul wrote to the Philippians that there is no more potent force on earth than the name of Jesus as it is used with faith by believers in Christ –

> *God also hath highly exalted him, and given him a name which is above every name:*
>
> *That at the name of Jesus every knee should bow, of things in heaven, and things in earth, and things under the earth;*
>
> *and that every tongue should confess that Jesus Christ is Lord, to the glory of God the Father*
>
> Philippians 2:9-11

• **No Problem Too Great.** We must never lose sight of the fact that Jesus was with the Father at creation. He knows how all things were made. John 1:3 tells us, "All things were made by him; and without him was not anything made that was made."

The One who has made all things knows how to *fix* all things when they are broken apart by either our sin or by the sinful nature of the world. The God who has created has the full power to re-create!

This is especially good news for those who find their marriages crumbling or in disarray. God knows how to bring the two of you back together. He has a healing solution for every ailment, no matter how great that ailment may be.

Our Glorious Inheritance

What a glorious inheritance we have as the "sons and daughters" of God Almighty, joint heirs with Jesus Christ! God has revealed Himself to us and called us to be His children – to grow up into His likeness. Our challenge is clear. We are to grow "in the unity of the faith, and of the knowledge of the Son of God" until we come to the state in which we are "a perfect man, unto the measure of the stature of the fullness of Christ" (Ephesians 4:13).

God not only calls us to this position, but He enables us to become the men and women that He calls us to be. The same is true in your marriage. God not only calls you to the wonderful opportunity of being a husband or wife, but He will enable you to fulfill your God-given role to the best of His ability.

Scriptures That Confirm:

We Have Power in the Name of Jesus

Go ye therefore, and teach all nations, baptizing them in the name of the Father, and of the Son, and of the Holy Ghost:

Teaching them to observe all things whatsoever I have commanded you: and, lo, I am with you alway, even unto the end of the world

Matthew 28:19-20

The seventy returned again with joy, saying, Lord, even the devils are subject unto us through thy name.

And he said unto them, I beheld Satan as lightning fall from heaven. Behold, I give unto you power to tread on serpents and scorpions, and over all the power of the enemy: and nothing shall by any means hurt you.

Notwithstanding in this rejoice not, that the spirits are

subject unto you; but rather rejoice, because your names are written in heaven

Luke 10:17-20

Whatsoever ye shall ask in my name, that will I do, that the Father may be glorified in the Son

John 14:13

In that day ye shall ask me nothing. Verily, verily, I say unto you, Whatsoever ye shall ask the Father in my name, he will give it you.

Hitherto have ye asked nothing in my name: ask, and ye shall receive, that your joy may be full

John 16:23-24

These are written, that ye might believe that Jesus is the Christ, the Son of God; and that believing ye might have life through his name

John 20:31

Peter said, Silver and gold have I none; but such as I have give I thee: In the name of Jesus Christ of Nazareth rise up and walk.

And he took him by the right hand, and lifted him up: and immediately his feet and ankle bones received strength.

And he leaping up stood, and walked, and entered with

them into the temple, walking, and leaping, and praising God

Acts 3:6-8

Peter said unto them, Repent, and be baptized every one of you in the name of Jesus Christ for the remission of sins, and ye shall receive the gift of the Holy Ghost

Acts 2:38

Ye are washed, but ye are sanctified, but ye are justified in the name of the Lord Jesus, and by the Spirit of our God

1 Corinthians 6:11

Wherefore God also hath highly exalted him, and given him a name which is above every name:

That at the name of Jesus every knee should bow, of things in heaven, and things in earth, and things under the earth:

and that every tongue should confess that Jesus Christ is Lord, to the glory of God the Father.

Wherefore, my beloved, as ye have always obeyed, not as in my presence only, but now much more in my absence, work out your own salvation with fear and trembling.

For it is God which worketh in you both to will and to do of his good pleasure

Philippians 2:9-13

Let the word of Christ dwell in you richly in all wisdom; teaching and admonishing one another in psalms and hymns and spiritual songs, singing with grace in your hearts to the Lord.

And whatsoever ye do in word or deed, do all in the name of the Lord Jesus, giving thanks to God and the Father by him

Colossians 3:16-17

I write unto you, little children, because your sins are forgiven you for his name's sake

1 John 2:12

He hath on his vesture and on his thigh a name written, King of Kings, and Lord of Lords

Revelation 19:16

CHAPTER 7

Chapter 7

Taking Your Spoken Words Seriously

Many times in life, we make idle statements. People sometimes seem to talk just for the sake of hearing themselves talk. The Bible teaches us that our words have importance and that we are to watch closely what we say.

Our salvation is related to a spoken confession of faith in Christ. In many ways, such a spoken confession may be likened to a vow. Romans 10:9 says –

> *If thou shalt confess with thy mouth the Lord Jesus, and shalt believe in thine heart that God hath raised him from the dead, thou shalt be saved.*

Confessing what we believe is a sign that we believe. From a very logical and practical standpoint, how is another person to know what you believe or feel unless you *tell* that person directly and in clear communication what you believe or feel.

Confession is not only a revelation of what we feel, however. It also acts as something of a *seal* to what we believe. Paul has said to the Romans that it isn't enough just to "believe" in Jesus' death and resurrection, but that we need to confess with our mouths our belief in Jesus Christ.

What does this mean to us as Christians? One thing it means is that when we say "Lord" we truly mean *Lord.* (See Matthew

7:21-23.) We must never use the name of the Lord lightly or claim to be following the Lord if we truly aren't willing to become a sold-out servant to whatever our Lord desires of us.

God is looking for people who will not only take their lives and their faith seriously, but who will take their words seriously. It is increasingly more difficult in our society, or so it seems, to find people who truly mean what they say and who say what they mean. We are a society that is continually looking for loopholes and means by which people can escape their commitments or justify their sins. God calls us to own up to our sins and to be continually searching for ways in which we can *fulfill* our vows, not duck them.

Neither are we to attempt to "add to" our vows after the fact. We are not to say, "Well, I said this, but actually what I meant was that." There were religious people who were doing just that in Jesus' time, adding oaths to some of their statements. Jesus said, "Let your communication be, Yea, yea; Nay, nay: for whatsoever is more than these cometh of evil" (Matthew 5:37). In other words, do what you say you will do, without embellishment or trying to gloss over what you know in your heart you are to do.

The very essence of a vow as opposed to a promise or pledge is that a vow is made in the presence of God with the full belief and assumption that God will enable you to *fulfill* that vow. A vow brings God in on the deal! It says to God, all present, and to yourself, "God is my full partner in bringing this vow to pass. I will work with Him and I know He will work with me."

The performance of vows is part of the vow-making itself. A spoken vow is only words; a vow in action is a genuine vow.

The Lord places great emphasis continually upon His people *doing* what they say they will do. Jesus said, "Why call ye me, Lord, Lord, and do not the things which I say?" (Luke 6:46). At the Last Supper, Jesus made it very clear to His disciples, "If a man love me, he will keep my words" (John 14:23), and "If ye keep my commandments, ye shall abide in my love" (John 15:10).

The Bible admonishes each of us, "Be ye doers of the word, and not hearers only" (James 1:22).

One of the key verses in the Bible that links our faith to our obedience is 1 John 3:22 – "And whatsoever we ask, we receive of him, because we keep his commandments, and do those things that are pleasing in his sight." It is by faith that we ask. It is in obedience that we receive!

God Honors Those Who Honor Vows

A story in the Bible that clearly demonstrates how much it pleases God for us to keep our word is the story of the Gibeonites. The Gibeonites were people who lived in the Promised Land at the time the children of Israel were about to enter that land and claim it as their God-given portion on the earth. The Israelites were under a divine command to wipe out all the peoples who stood in their path, including the Gibeonites.

The Gibeonites heard of the advancing Israelites and they developed a plan to fool Joshua. They sent ambassadors to Joshua dressed in ragged clothing and with old, stale food. They made themselves appear to be from a faraway land. In this, they tricked Israel into making a covenant with them so that they might not be destroyed. Joshua 9:15 tells us, "Joshua made peace with them, and made a league with them, to let them live: and the princes of the congregation sware unto them."

Now even though this covenant was forged on the basis of a lie, and even though the real truth was in direct contradiction to what God had ordered, Israel was under an obligation before God to honor its spoken commitment to the Gibeonites. Why? Because covenant is based upon what is said, not on what another person does.

When the Gibeonites were faced with an attack from five kings, they called upon their covenant brothers for help, and because of the covenant they had made, Joshua and his men came to their aid. In Joshua 10:9-11 we read –

> *Joshua therefore came unto them suddenly, and went up from Gilgal all night.*
>
> *And the Lord discomfited them before Israel, and slew them with a great slaughter at Gibeon, and chased them along the way that goeth up to Beth-horon, and smote them to Azekah, and unto Makkedah.*
>
> *And it came to pass, as they fled from before Israel, and were in the going down to Beth-horon, that the Lord cast down great stones from heaven upon them unto Azekah, and they died: they were more which died from hailstones than they whom the children of Israel slew with the sword.*

God chose sides in this battle on behalf of the very people that He had previously told the Israelites to destroy. Why? Because of the covenant agreement His people had made! God stood by the covenant. One of the greatest miracles in all the Bible occurred during this very battle – the miracle in which the sun stood still and the moon stayed until the victory was complete. There has never been a day like it before or since.

God stood behind His people even when they were in support of a covenant that had been made in deception.

You and your spouse may not have known fully what you

were "vowing" to each other when you made your marriage vows before God. In some ways, you may have been deceiving yourself, or perhaps even deceiving your spouse. Even so, God stands with you to help you fulfill your covenant *as you vowed it,* not as you understood it.

This is a very important concept for you to understand. God will help you stand by your vows even though you may not have fully understood the meaning of your vows at the time you made them. He will help you do the right thing – which is to do what you said you would do.

Voicing a Renewal of Your Vows

We all know that in order to have a good relationship with another person, we need to be able to communicate well. Part of that communication, of course, is the ability to listen intently and accurately. Part is being able to communicate accurately. But there is yet another part: what we feel and think we need to put into spoken words. Many a spouse has said, "I thought you knew how I felt." In reality, the other spouse had never *heard* any words that conveyed such a feeling!

It's important that you tell your spouse on a regular basis, "I love you." No person ever tires of hearing that message when it is spoken genuinely and with heartfelt warmth. You also need to tell your spouse when you are hurting. Many people try to "stuff" all negative emotions. They think that to admit them to another person makes them a wimp, cry-baby, complainer, or even a manipulator or person of judgment and condemnation. The better alternative is to say how you feel *without* any motive of judgment or manipulation. An honest expression of feelings, rooted in truth and spoken in love, is always more helpful than harmful in the long run. A person can't change his behavior, seek to make amends or ask forgiveness, if he doesn't know he has made a mistake or error.

Your spouse cannot read your mind, or your heart. He or she will not know that you are forgiving him or her *unless you say so.* He will not know why you are doing many of the things you do, *unless you say so.* She will not know what you are trying to accomplish, *unless you say so.*

Just as your vows at your marriage were not *thought* only but were words spoken out loud, so the ongoing renewal of your vows must not only be thought and felt, but spoken. Your spouse needs to hear that you still care, still love, still desire, still dream, still believe, still are interested.

Learn to speak how you feel without letting long periods of time elapse before you first have a feeling and the time you speak. If you hold on to feelings of any kind – negative or positive, they can escalate over time into something that comes across to another person as being strident, extreme, or unfounded.

These same principles, of course, are ones that directly apply to prayer and our communication with God. We must be completely open and honest with the Lord about our feelings. He knows how we feel – the benefit of expression is entirely ours. It is far better to vent our feelings than to keep them bottled up where they can turn into deep bitterness or anger.

We also need to learn to pray "sooner" rather than "later" when we sense that things are going awry in our lives or in our marriages. Don't wait for the problem or conflict to become monumental. Pray about the small things as they arise. And whenever possible, pray together about potential problems that you see could arise in your family or which could impact your marriage.

Making Your Desire Known to God

Many times in the Scriptures we find places where the Lord asked those in need to *state* what it was that they desired. This is not because the Lord didn't already know – surely He knows all things. (He knows precisely what you need right now!) Rather, this requirement of the Lord is so that we might hear from our own lips *precisely what it is that we desire the Lord to do for us.*

Do you know what you desire from the Lord today? Are you able to express it in concise, precise terms?

It is not enough to say, "Well, I want a better marriage." Better in what ways?

It is not enough to say, "I want my husband to come back to me." Come back and do what? Live how? As he was or as a changed person? To the same environment or a different one? To the old you or to a new and spiritually improved you?

It is not enough to say, "I desire a change in my marriage." What kind of change? Who is going to change and in what ways? Why a change?

We must be very specific when we express ourselves to the Lord. Otherwise, we aren't really sure how to apply our faith. In other words, if you don't know what you are believing for precisely, then your believing is less effective. It is unfocused and in many ways, scattered or diluted.

Faith is given to us to use in precise ways, like a sharp scalpel toward the removal of those things which are sinful, diseased, unhealthful, harmful, and disobedient. Faith is also given to us to use like a sharp sickle – so that we might reap precisely what we need.

Verbalizing Your Faith. The Lord expects His people to verbalize their faith – not only to put what they believe, and what they are believing for, into words, but then to *speak those words aloud.* Read what Jesus said –

> *Verily I say unto you, that whosoever shall say unto this mountain, Be thou removed, and be thou cast into the sea; and shall not doubt in his heart, but shall believe that those things which he saith shall come to pass; he shall have whatsoever he saith.*
>
> *Therefore I say unto you, What things soever ye desire, when ye pray, believe that ye receive them, and ye shall have them*
>
> Mark 11:23–24;
> (underlines added for emphasis)

There are a number of words in the New Testament that refer to speaking, one of which is "confess." Confession is made verbally and audibly. In James 5:16 we read, "Confess your faults one to another, and pray one for another, that ye may be healed." In 1 John 1:9 we read, "If we confess our sins, he is faithful and just to forgive us our sins, and to cleanse us from all unrighteousness."

Many a marriage could be healed and strengthened if both partners in the marriage chose to "confess their faults" to one another and to seek forgiveness and help. This must always be done, however, in the spirit of helping, not hurting, the other person.

Mack knew that he had not spent as much time with his wife Fran as she would have liked. He knew that he had been inconsiderate to her on a number of occasions, and had even criticized her unfairly before others. Although he had apologized to her many times, he also knew that his apologies were beginning to sound like "just so many words."

Mack wisely took a closer look at his life. He realized that much of his critical attitude was a reflection of the attitude he had perceived from his parents, especially his father. He realized also that his strong work drive, which caused him to spend many more hours in the busy-ness of work than were actually required to get his job done, was also a carryover from his father's behavior. Mack asked the Lord's forgiveness and opened himself to the Lord's healing power. Then he went to Fran and said, "I realize that this is who I have become and I don't want to be this person. I don't want to be so driven or so critical and inconsiderate. Please forgive me for being this way to you on so many occasions. Please help me to become the person I know God wants me to be."

Fran was deeply touched by Mack's "confession" to her. She readily forgave him and then sought gentle, beneficial ways of helping Mack to become less of a workaholic and less demanding of himself and others. Mack continued to succeed in his work, almost to his surprise since he was putting in fewer but more productive hours. He also began to succeed in new ways in his relationship with Fran. He discovered that praise and appreciation were far more potent than any form of criticism or demand!

Be Specific in What You Say

We are called by God to be very specific in stating to the Lord what we desire for Him to do on our behalf.

A blind man once came to Jesus. He had a blind man's vacant stare, he acted blind as he stumbled toward Jesus with his cane, and he was dressed like a blind beggar. Jesus readily could tell that this man was blind. There was no doubt about it! Yet Jesus asked him, "What do you want me to do for you?" (See Mark 10:51.)

The more specific you are, the easier it will be for you to tell when the Lord answers your prayer and the easier it will be for you to believe and do *your part* toward seeing a desired change.

A pastor in a counseling session once asked a woman, "You say that you want your husband to change, but in what ways do you want him to change?"

She said, "Well, I want him to change his whole attitude toward our marriage. I want him to be involved in the home and with the children."

The pastor asked again, "What specifically do you want him to do?"

She said, "I want him to spend more time with the children and to do more of the household chores."

The pastor asked yet again, "What specifically do you mean by more time? What specific chores do you have in mind?"

She replied, "I want him to spend at least thirty minutes a day with our children, and I want him to take out the trash."

The pastor insisted, "What do you want him to do during those thirty minutes with your children and when do you want him to take out the trash?"

She said, "I want him to spend thirty minutes a day helping our children with their homework and reading them a bedtime story and saying prayers with them by their bedside. I want him to take the trash can out to the street on Monday and Thursday nights."

The pastor said, "Now that's a start! That's something we can agree about together in prayer. Tell your husband those specific things that you desire for him to do. Express your pleasure to him when he does those things for you. See what happens."

Two things happened. First, when the husband heard *specifically* what his wife desired for him to do, he said, "Sure, if you had only told me what you wanted me to do, I would have been happy to do that all along. I didn't know what you wanted." On the wife's part, she made it easy for him to fulfill his role. She had the trash all bundled up. She had the table cleared and the children seated at it ready for their father's input on their homework; then she got the children bathed and ready to hear a Bible story and say prayers. The husband felt fulfilled in his new role as a helper.

The second thing that happened was that the wife thanked her husband repeatedly for doing these things in their home and with their children. He felt increasingly more appreciated and a more valuable member of the family. He felt more needed, more important to his children, and more a part of the ongoing life of the family. He had been given a role to fill and he found pleasure in filling that role.

The pastor asked the wife some time later, "What is it that you want in your marriage?"

The wife replied, "Oh, things are going great. There are lots of things my husband has started doing that I wouldn't even have dreamed to ask. He is going to church and Sunday school with us as a family, and he is much more affectionate to me and to the children. Everything has changed."

But it started with taking out the trash can to the street on Mondays and Thursdays, and with spending thirty minutes of time each evening with his children doing homework, reading a Bible story, and saying good-night prayers.

Be specific. Your faith will be more energized if you have a very direct and limited goal in mind.

• **Steps and Degrees of Change.** Don't try to take on a massive mountain of change. Choose something small that you desire to see changed. Recognize that change is a process.

Believe for isolated, discrete, yet meaningful changes. Find a part that you can play in helping to make the change easier or to help bring about the change.

A bride named Elsie married a man whom she loved a great deal and he loved her a great deal in return. But he was a man who didn't bathe regularly. As a result, Elsie found it difficult to be close to him. The body odor was repulsive to her and although she loved her husband greatly, she found it very difficult to be intimate with him on occasion. He, in turn, felt rejected and hurt by her lack of physical response to him.

Elsie began to believe God for a change – and specifically, that her husband would bathe regularly. As she prayed for her husband and about this change she desired in her marriage, the Lord revealed to her a few very simple steps to take and she obeyed.

First, she bought a new shower head that had a number of settings on it – including a massage setting. She also purchased a bottle of cologne and put it on her husband's dresser with a little note that said, "Just for you. No special occasion. Just because I love you."

One evening her husband found her reading a book on how a wife might give a massage to her husband. He found the idea intriguing. She replied that a massage with the oils that she had purchased with the book was better accomplished if a person had just bathed in hot water and the pores were open. He quickly moved to take a shower! And when he did, he found a new and interesting shower head in his shower.

This young man quickly developed a new hygiene habit, one that included cologne and massages!

But, you may say, is this an act of faith? Yes! All the while, this woman was believing God for a change. It was the Lord who revealed to her the simple steps she took. She obeyed the Lord and trusted Him to make her husband receptive to a new pattern of hygiene in his life. She made her gifts to her husband in love and in faith. She responded to him at all times with generosity and with a desire for what was best for him and for their marriage.

The old saying is true: "It's the little things that add up." This is true in our faith and in our giving, just as in other areas of life. A relationship is always a composite of actions, of moments, of behaviors, or conversations.

A man once told a friend that he felt the secret to their fifty-year marriage was this: "I agreed to handle the big things and my wife agreed to handle the little things." The wife quickly added, "But what I came to realize more than forty-nine years ago was that if I handled all the little things, there were no big things left for him to handle!"

As you see God work in the "little things" to which you apply your faith and your love, your faith and your love will grow. You will feel encouraged. You will find it natural to believe God for greater things. You will find it easy to show greater expressions of love.

Your Spoken Words Shape Your Destiny

The importance of staying true to one's vows over time is the theme of a very brief but potent story in the Bible. In Jeremiah 35:2 we read about an experience that the prophet Jeremiah had with the Rechabites: "Go unto the house of the Rechabites, and speak unto them, and bring them into the house of the Lord, into one of the chambers, and give them wine to drink."

Jeremiah did as God had commanded. To his surprise, when he set pots of wine and cups before the Rechabites, they refused to drink. They said to Jeremiah, "We will drink no wine: for Jonadab the son of Rechab our father commanded us, saying, Ye shall drink no wine, neither ye, nor your sons for ever: . . . that ye may live many days in the land where ye be strangers. Thus have we obeyed the voice of Jonadab" (Jeremiah 35:6–8).

God used this commitment of the Rechabites to illustrate to Jeremiah the kind of people that God chooses to bless. The Rechabites had remained faithful to what they knew to be God's command to them through their ancestor Jonadab for *three hundred years!* God spoke through Jeremiah that someone from this family would stand before God forever. What a blessing for remaining true to what you know to be God's command! (See Jeremiah 35:19.)

Our spoken words shape our destiny. Once we have committed ourselves to a pledge, vow, or a statement of belief, our subsequent actions become a statement of either compliance or noncompliance with what we have said. Our actions say to others that we lie or speak the truth. To a great extent, we are responsible for carrying out what it is that we say *the moment that we speak.*

Our spoken words also shape our relationships. How many relationships have been harmed by one misspoken statement! James referred to this when he wrote –

> *We all stumble in many ways. If anyone is never at fault in what he says, he is a perfect man, able to keep his whole body in check.*
>
> *When we put bits into the mouths of horses to make them obey us, we can turn the whole animal.*
>
> *Or take ships as an example. Although they are so large*

and are driven by strong winds, they are steered by a very small rudder wherever the pilot wants to go.

Likewise the tongue is a small part of the body, but it makes great boasts. Consider what a great forest is set on fire by a small spark

James 3:2-5 (NIV)

Watch what you say. Refuse to speak in anger or out of hatred, prejudice, or hurt feelings to another person. Check your feelings and evaluate what it is that is most beneficial for you to say — not only for yourself, but also for the other person and your relationship with that person. While it is important to express feelings, it is not helpful to express feelings that are unbridled by wisdom. God can handle hearing anything from you. Vent to Him! Then ask Him to help you express your feelings to another person in a way that is pleasing to Him! Trust Him to give you the words to say and also the right attitude for expressing them.

Scriptures That Confirm:

Our Spoken Words Have Great Power

If ye abide in me, and my words abide in you, ye shall ask what ye will, and it shall be done unto you

John 15:7

Whatsoever ye shall ask of the Father in my name, he may give it you

John 15:16

Hitherto have ye asked nothing in my name: ask, and ye shall receive, that your joy may be full

John 16:24

Chapter 8

Chapter 8

Commitment to a Relationship Lies Beyond "Keeping the Rules"

No Christian ever enters any relationship alone. We may *think* we are entering a relationship "on our own" but if we are Christians, that is not the case. We enter every relationship *with God accompanying us.* The Holy Spirit resides in us. He moves where we move. He lives where we live. We are vessels that He fills and occupies, and from which He does not depart.

Therefore, when we enter a relationship with another person, we enter it *in Christ* and *with Christ* because the very Spirit of Christ indwells us.

This is a vital concept for you to grasp. When you make a vow to another person that is in line with God's Word, both you and God simultaneously have entered a covenant relationship with that person!

God will not turn His back on a covenant relationship. He will not go back on His Word. He will not turn His back on a person with whom He has made a covenant.

Indeed, the foremost purpose of covenant is to bring mankind into a *relationship* with God so that God might impart His power into the lives of His people – to bring them salvation, deliverance, blessings, healing, restoration, and miracles.

A Desire for Relationship

God desires relationship. It was out of that motivation that God created man and woman initially. It is from that motivation that we see the great redemptive acts of God through the ages. It is because God desires relationship that He has made provision for man's salvation from pain, suffering, and death – spiritually as well as physically and emotionally. Many of the most famous and most moving stories of the Bible are built around this theme.

The story of Ruth in the Bible is one of great courage and character, but it is also a story that is motivated by a desire for relationship. Ruth, as a Moabitess, was a member of a group that generally was despised by the Jews. Ruth's husband died and her mother-in-law, Naomi – a Jewess – decided to return home. Ruth, in her desire for relationship with both Naomi and Naomi's God, committed herself to return with Naomi. She spoke some of the most heartfelt and meaningful words of commitment to relationship that we see in the Bible –

> *Intreat me not to leave thee, or to return from following after thee: for whither thou goest, I will go; and where thou lodgest, I will lodge: thy people shall be my people, and thy God my God:*
>
> *Where thou diest, will I die, and there will I be buried: the Lord do so to me, and more also, if ought but death part thee and me*
>
> Ruth 1:16-17

As the result of Ruth committing herself so completely to Naomi, blessings began to occur in her life. At first, it was a blessing of just a little extra grain that Boaz had his laborers leave for her as she gleaned in his fields. But it was not long before Boaz, a rich but distant relative of Naomi, proposed marriage to Ruth. Later, she bore a son who became the grandfather to King David, and thus, Ruth became a part of the lineage of Jesus!

The theme of relationship is also strong in the book of Job, who was so committed to his faith in God that he declared, "Though he slay me, yet will I trust in him" (Job 13:15). Although it must have seemed to Job that he was attacked by hell itself and deserted by God, Job chose to remain true to two things: his integrity and his commitment to believing God. Years of blessing followed his time of trial.

In calling His disciples to Himself, Jesus was looking for one main character trait: the ability to commit. His command to His apostles was simple: "Follow Me." Those who did so often left their jobs and homes to be with Him for prolonged periods of time. Through difficult times when Jesus' teachings were difficult to understand and His popularity seemed to be on the decline, the apostles stayed close to Jesus. Simon Peter spoke on their behalf in this poignant scene in the Gospel of John –

> *From that time many of his disciples went back, and walked no more with him.*
>
> *Then said Jesus unto the twelve, Will ye also go away?*
>
> *Then Simon Peter answered him, Lord, to whom shall we go? thou hast the words of eternal life.*
>
> *And we believe and are sure that thou art that Christ, the Son of the living God*
>
> John 6:66-69

To the apostles, relationship with Jesus meant everything.

Beyond a Matter of "Keeping the Rules"

Living in a covenant relationship requires far more than just "keeping the rules." It requires ongoing faith in God and including God in all areas of one's life.

Paul made it very clear that we cannot have a relationship with Christ by "keeping the rules." Our relationship is rooted in faith and faith alone. In Galatians 3:10–11 we read –

> *Yes, and those who depend on the Jewish laws to save them are under God's curse, for the Scriptures point out very clearly, "Cursed is everyone who at any time breaks a single one of these laws that are written in God's Book of the Law."*
>
> *Consequently, it is clear that no one can ever win God's favor by trying to keep the Jewish laws, because God has said that the only way we can be right in his sight is by faith*
>
> (TLB)

As the prophet Habakkuk said, "The man who finds life will find it through trusting God." How different from this way of faith is the way of law, which says that a man is saved by obeying every law of God, without one slip.

Not By Works But By Faith

To say that we can hold a marriage together, make a marriage good, or restore a failing marriage to health is to say that "by works" we can achieve a good marriage. Keeping the rules is just another way of saying "doing the works." Nothing is saved, salvaged, healed, restored, or built into something lasting and of value through "works."

No person was ever saved by keeping outward rules of righteousness, although countless people have certainly tried! So many churches have "rules" of various kinds that are expected to keep a person on the straight and narrow path – for example, don't have long hair (for men), don't have short hair (for women), don't dance, don't drink, don't smoke, don't, don't, don't, don't. Those who keep these rules diligently often do so out of fear that if they fail to "keep the rules" they will lose their salvation, or even more in error, out of a hope that if they do "keep the rules" they will gain their salvation.

Other churches have "do rules" – do belong to this committee, do serve on this board or in this ministry, do attend church. While these are all very good activities, if the motive is that one will "achieve" a relationship with God by doing them, the motive is wrong.

The same pattern extends to marriage. There are those who have a fixed idea of what must be done by the wife, or done by the husband, in order for a marriage to work. A wife may work hard to "do, do, do" all that she thinks is required, only to find that her marriage is crumbling around her. A husband, likewise, can find himself wondering, ***What went wrong? I did everything a good husband is supposed to do.*** In like manner, a husband or wife may find themselves saying, "But I never once did such and such," and think that because they didn't do something, their marriage should have been troublefree.

That rarely is the case.

Relationships are living, breathing entities. The rules governing marriage are actually very few from a Scriptural standpoint –

- Husbands are to love their wives as they love themselves They are to show honor to their wives. (See 1 Peter 3:7.)

· A husband is to be the spiritual "head" of his wife, yet he is never to use this position for domineering power plays – rather he is to love as Christ loved and to give himself completely to his wife. The position of leadership is to be a supreme position of service. (See Ephesians 5:23,25–26.)

· Wives are to honor and submit themselves to their husbands in areas of decision-making for the family and in matters related to spiritual guidance for the family. While a wife is to be submissive, she is never to use her submission as a tool of manipulation. She is to submit to her husband in the same spirit as she submits to the Lord. (See Ephesians 5:22.)

· Husbands are to attempt to understand their wives and to give honor to them, recognizing that their wives are joint heirs with them in Christ. (Seel Peter 3:7.)

· Wives are to be chaste and in obedience to their husbands so that they might build up their husbands in their commitment to the Lord. (Seel Peter 3:1-6.)

· Both husbands and wives are to be faithful to each other sexually. (See Exodus 20:14.)

Anything other than these basic scriptural guidelines is always to flow out of a couple's communication and mutual understanding. At no time in Scripture, for example, do we find that "wives must cook" or "husbands must take out the trash."

In Susan and Chuck's marriage, Susan mows the lawn and Chuck runs the vacuum cleaner. Susan loves the outdoors and Chuck suffers from an allergy to grass. This division of labor works for them.

In Mary and Bill's marriage, Mary runs errands on her way home from work while Bill fixes dinner each night. Mary's route to work takes her past many of the services that the family needs – dry cleaners, shoe repair shop, and so forth – while Bill works at home and finds it easy to put meals together. This division of labor works for them.

All matters related to chores in maintaining a home fall into the category of "to be decided" by a couple. There are no set rules or commandments that govern this area of marriage.

The important aspect to the marriage is the relationship. Can the two people in a marriage talk through how they want to live? Can they find agreement in how they make decisions and come to conclusions that will govern their life together?

No Guarantees Related to "Works." Furthermore, there are no guarantees that if one person does all that is expected of him or her that a marriage will flourish. What causes a marriage to flourish is having a vibrant, living, loving relationship. And only God can breathe life and love into a relationship, just as only God can breathe life and love into a person's body or spirit. As the prophet Jeremiah said, "They shall be my people, and I will be their God: And I will give them one heart, and one way, that they may fear me for ever, for the good of them, and of their children after them" (Jeremiah 32:38-39). The creation of one heart and one way is God's work. We must continue to trust God for the ingredients that only God can give to a marriage. He is the sustainer of all that is living and growing – marriages included!

Vern operated under the assumption that to make his wife happy, he needed to earn as much money as possible so that he could provide the best quality of life for her and their children. In order to earn as much money as possible, of course, he had to work overtime, and eventually, he even took on a second job in order to provide even more for his wife.

One day Vern came home to find his wife Barbara in tears.

When he asked her what was bothering her, she took the next two hours to tell him! Vern had no idea until that evening that Barbara had been the least bit dissatisfied with their marriage.

What was it that Barbara had wanted from Vern that she was not receiving? Time. She missed the days when they could go for evening walks together or sit by the fireplace and talk. She missed weekends in which they could be together and enjoy a leisurely Saturday brunch and spend extra time with friends on Sunday afternoon. Vern pointed out that if he didn't work overtime or his weekend job, they couldn't continue to have such nice things. Barbara made it very clear that she didn't want things . . . she wanted Vern.

Vern actually found it a relief to give up the overtime hours and his second job. He not only had more time but also more emotional energy to give to Barbara. In the next year, Vern and Barbara moved to a smaller house, gave up some of the luxuries they had acquired – such as country-club memberships and dining out at expensive restaurants – and in the process, they enjoyed a much higher quality of life and marriage.

Keeping the rule of "being a good provider" monetarily and materially was replaced with a higher law of being a good "provider" of emotional and spiritual support! The drive to be a financial success had been a burden; the desire to be in relationship was not a burden, but a joy.

The Holy Spirit Enables Us in Our Relationships

It is Jesus Christ living in us, in the form of the Holy Spirit, who gives us the power to do the will of God. It is the Holy Spirit who transforms our very desires and our thoughts so that they are in line with the covenant relationship God desires for us to have with Him and with our spouse. We must trust the Holy Spirit on a daily basis to help us live the life that God has designed for our good.

"Keeping the rules" doesn't guarantee a good life, a good marriage, or a good relationship with God. "Keeping in relationship with the Holy Spirit" does!

Paul wrote about this, saying –

> *For what the law was powerless to do in that it was weakened by the sinful nature, God did by sending his own Son in the likeness of sinful man to be a sin offering. And so he condemned sin in sinful man,*
>
> *in order that the righteous requirements of the law might be fully met in us, who do not live according to the sinful nature but according to the Spirit*
>
> Romans 8:3–4 (NIV)

Coming to Want What God Wants

It is out of relationship that we come to learn what it is that God truly desires for our lives, individually and personally. Intimacy of relationship with God reveals to us God's heartbeat and His deepest will. We cannot ignore a daily ongoing relationship with God and then expect that when we come to God in "crisis mode" that God will automatically reveal to us His deepest desires and plans. We must ask God daily for guidance and direction, so that we truly might walk in His ways and live in accordance with His will.

Mike had absolutely no doubts that Ginger was the woman for him. He had dated her for four months and he was sure he wanted to marry her – he couldn't imagine a better wife. When Mike told his pastor his intent to marry Ginger, the pastor asked him a key question, "Can you be a good husband to Ginger?"

Mike answered "yes" very quickly but upon later reflection, he realized that he had never given serious thought to that question or its answer. He had focused entirely on what kind of wife he felt Ginger would be to *him,* not on what kind of husband he would be to her.

Shortly after this encounter with his pastor, Mike had a conversation with his uncle, who asked him, "Have you talked to God about marrying Ginger?" Mike had to admit that he hadn't. He had assumed that because everything seemed so "right" between them as they had dated that Ginger *must* be an acceptable choice of a spouse to God.

Mike began to pray in earnest, asking God to show him if there was anything that he needed to know about Ginger, or anything he needed to change in the way he related to Ginger. As he prayed, Mike felt the Lord revealing to him several areas in which Mike was not prepared to be a husband. He also felt impressed that there were some areas of need in Ginger's life that neither of them had addressed, although he didn't know precisely what they might be.

After they had dated for nine months, Ginger revealed to Mike that she had been sexually molested as a child and that she still had many fears and emotional problems related to that experience. She also revealed that she had both an eating disorder and an overspending habit that very likely were related to her molestation as a child. She told Mike that she didn't believe she should continue dating him until after she had received adequate help from a professional Christian psychologist.

Mike found it difficult to let Ginger "go" so that she might receive help without his influence in her life, but he agreed to part ways with her. He continued to pray for Ginger and to seek

God about a marriage to her. The more he prayed, however, the more Mike felt a release in his spirit regarding Ginger.

About six months after Ginger had broken off their relationship, Mike met a girl named Amy. This time, from their first date onward, Mike prayed diligently about dating Amy. Over the course of a yearlong courtship, the Lord increasingly directed Mike that *this* was the girl Mike should marry and with whom he truly could have a covenant marriage.

Initially, Amy had not been at all the "kind of girl" that Mike had thought he would one day marry. But the more he got to know Amy, the more he saw in her the traits and qualities that blended well with his own personality and gifts. He had a deep respect for her faith. Certainly Amy had experienced problems in her life as well, but at the time she met Mike, she had worked her way through those problems in faith and prayer.

It was when Mike came to want what *God* wanted in his life that he truly found the woman with whom he could enter a lifelong relationship.

Many couples find themselves married before they face up to their differences and their own personal problems. Even so, the Lord can help them come to the place where they will want what God wants.

Genuine Submission to God's Plan

Patricia's story of obedience to God's plan is quite different. For years, Patricia felt that she had to prove herself equal to her husband in all ways. In fact, she was quite competitive with her husband. If he got a raise, she sought a raise to an equal or greater salary than his. If he won an award, she sought to win an award of equal value in her career. If her husband wanted to go on a hunting trip as a vacation, she sought "equal time" to go on a shopping trip with her friends. Equality was a major word in Patricia's vocabulary.

Any time a Bible study, Sunday school lesson, or sermon bordered on the subject of submission – not only submission of wives to husbands in decision-making matters, but more general submission of one to another in the body of Christ – Patricia either got up and walked out of the room or she attempted to argue her position of absolute equality.

When Patricia and her husband Jerry began to have problems in their marriage, however, Patricia took no part of the fault for herself. Equal success? Yes. Equal in contributing to the problems? No.

Although Patricia did not see herself as having fault in her life, she also didn't want to lose her husband, whom she genuinely loved. She sought out a Christian counselor when her husband mentioned the possibility of a legal separation.

The counselor addressed Patricia's difficulties with the word "submission" and attempted to correct some of the bad teaching that Patricia had received in her life. Patricia had grown up believing that submission meant to be a doormat. When she saw that submission related to specific courses of action and a decision-making role, she felt somewhat better, but not completely. When she told her longtime and faithful friend Evelyn about one particular session with her counselor, Evelyn said in exasperation, "Oh, Patricia, give it a try. A little submission wouldn't hurt you. You are always so concerned about being right or being the 'best.' Maybe submission to Jerry is the best plan for your marriage." Patricia was startled, and somewhat angered, at her friend's statements. She began to think, however, about what her friend had said – *What if submission is BEST?*

Patricia realized the more she thought about submission that she really hadn't submitted herself completely to God. She had accepted Christ Jesus as her Savior, but she had never really yielded to Him as Lord of her life. She had still tried to maintain control in a number of areas. She repented of this and asked the Lord to take complete control of her life. She felt a tremendous release, and she later asked the Lord to help her in submission to Jerry.

At first, Patricia put a number of qualifiers on her role as a submissive wife – things such as "if Jerry is in your will," "if he truly knows what to do," and "if his way is the right way." Again, the Lord revealed to her in prayer that this was not truly a submissive attitude, but a "compromise and negotiate" position. It took a great deal of effort for Patricia to begin to have a submissive heart.

One of the things that Patricia realized very quickly, however, as she truly related to Jerry in a submissive way regarding spiritual decisions, was that Jerry very rarely sought a way that was different than Patricia's own opinion. Another thing she discovered was that Jerry could sense the change in her attitude and he responded to it by demonstrating greater courage and strength than she had seen in him before. She liked the change she saw.

A third thing she discovered was that the more she yielded to Jerry in matters related to their mutual life together, the more Jerry sought out her opinion before he made a final decision. She actually had more input into their marriage and life together than she had before.

What happened to Patricia was not an outward change as much as it was an inward change – a change of her heart to come into line with God's plan. That inward change built up relationship. It destroyed the competitive atmosphere that had existed between Patricia and Jerry.

When competition is allowed to exist in a relationship, rules must also exist because competition requires "rules of play." The more Patricia turned away from the competitive rules that she had instilled into her marriage, the more she was able to embrace God's greater rule of love and submission one to another. Relationship was built up rather than torn down.

The Holy Spirit always works within us, and within our marriages, to build us up in Christ Jesus. He does not diminish the excellence of our potential or our future, but rather, expands our capacity to reflect Christ to others.

Your Marriage Is a Gift from God

None of us can *achieve* anything relationally on our own strength or charm. We certainly cannot establish a relationship with God on the basis of what we have done – rather, our relationship with God is always established on the basis of what God has done and said.

We are in no position to come before God with a proud strut, saying, "I am a popular, talented person, and You need me." The reality is, we need God. Our personalities, talents, and achievements – including our involvement in "church work" – cannot save us or put us into right relationship with God.

This same principle extends to our marriages. They are a gift of God to us initially, and the maintenance of a good marriage requires that God be allowed to do His work in each partner. None of us is in a position to brag about what a good marriage we have achieved, or to claim that we can have a good relationship with a spouse by keeping a few rules and hoping that counts for something. A truly good marriage *from God's perspective* occurs only when two people desire to have a marriage and they allow God to be a part of their lives and their marriage. God's desire for marriage is covenant and a marriage covenant cannot fully be established apart from God.

Many people find themselves on a merry-go-round, of sorts. They try to keep God's commandments, then fail to keep one or more of the commandments, and then try by their own efforts to "climb aboard" once again and keep the commandments, only to fail again, try again, fail again, and so on. The fact is, without God's help, none of us can keep God's commandments – including those related to marriage. Without His ongoing assistance, none of us can be successful in keeping our covenant relationships.

The Enemy of Pride. Those who think they can maintain a good relationship with either God or their spouse on their own efforts are generally guilty of pride. They believe it is within their power, without any assistance from God or others, to achieve whatever they desire to achieve, including a relationship with a marriage partner. They are sorely wrong.

Radine had very specific things that she had grown up believing were the "right" things to do to keep a husband happy. These were things that her mother had not sought to teach Radine, but rather, were things that Radine "picked up" from observing her mother. She had no reason to question these things since her mother had been married to her father for twenty-six years by the time Radine married.

These four things were at the top of Radine's list: keep an immaculate house, dress well, never work outside the home (to show dependence upon her husband), and go to church every Sunday morning.

When Radine's husband, David, left her for another woman, Radine was in a state of shock. She asked David, "Didn't I keep a nice home? Didn't you like the way I dressed? Didn't you say you wanted a wife who would stay at home with the children and go to church with you on Sunday?" David agreed that Radine had done all those things. Nevertheless, he left.

Radine was further stunned when she learned more about the woman who David was dating. This woman, whom we will call Sue, was not a good housekeeper, tended to dress very casually and somewhat offbeat, had a fulltime job at a bookstore, and although she went to church frequently, she was not known for every-Sunday attendance. Radine could not see what David saw in her!

The main point, however, is that Radine never asked David what he saw in this other woman. Neither had she ever asked David what was important to *him* in the marriage. She had simply assumed that what she saw as the criteria for a perfect marriage were the "right" criteria for all people in all marriages.

Had Radine asked David, she would have learned that what David valued most was a wife who had dinner waiting for him when he got home (or at least was in the process of preparing it), praised him more than criticized him, wasn't an overspender, and was genuinely interested in what he had thought, said, or done during any given day.

For her part, Radine had detested cooking, had been very critical of David for not making more money, spent the family into debt, and rarely asked David when he arrived home, "How was your day?" In sum, what David needed was not at all what Radine had sought to provide. She was totally self-absorbed in doing what she perceived to be necessary to be a good wife. Although Radine might have said she was keeping house, dressing well, and so forth for her husband's benefit, in truth she was doing these things for herself.

When a person is that self-centered and self-absorbed, pride is at work. The person is thinking only about what he or she wants, rather than what might be helpful or encouraging to his or her spouse.

This prideful attitude can show up in our relationship with the Lord, too. When we begin to say to God, "Look at all I am doing for You!" rather than praising God, saying, "I'm so thankful and in awe for all that You do for me" we are in serious trouble.

It is not what we *do* that keeps a relationship healthy, but rather, it is doing those things that the other person desires that keeps a relationship whole. God desires our praise and thanksgiving – He tells us that this is the way we are to come into His presence. (See Psalm 100:4.) God desires that we communicate with Him in prayer and that we tell others about His love and forgiveness. God desires that we obey Him when He asks us to do something, say something, or undertake a special mission that He authorizes. When we follow our own agenda, we are doing what we desire, not necessarily what God desires.

Ask your spouse what is important to your *spouse* in your marriage. Ask the Lord what is important to Him in your relationship with Him!

Our Relationship to the Commandments of God. In realizing that we cannot keep the commandments of God on our own strength, we must avoid the tendency to think, Well, if I can't keep the commandments anyway, why even try? At no time are we given a license to ignore God's commandments, cease trying to keep them, or to diminish their importance. We are never given any type of "license to sin" by God.

Juan was a man who grew up hearing stories and being teased about being "Don Juan." He felt he had to live up to his namesake reputation. He lived a life of great sexual immorality from the time he was sixteen until he married in his late twenties.

Even after he came to know Christ Jesus as his Savior, Juan had a great deal of difficulty controlling his sexual desires. When he married, he said to his wife, "Don't expect me to be faithful to you sexually. Just know that I love you most and I married you."

Deep inside Juan knew that he *should* be faithful to his wife but he had spent years convincing himself that he had a sexual drive that no one woman could satisfy. He reasoned, "God made me this way so this is the way I am and will be."

Juan's wife, Leticia, could not tolerate his infidelity, but neither did she want to divorce the man she loved and with whom she considered herself to be in covenant relationship. She began to pray in earnest for Juan, and every morning when Juan left for work, Leticia said to him, "I love you and I'm going to be praying for you all day that God will help you be faithful to me."

Was Juan faithful to his wife? Yes!

The more he was faithful and experienced the power of the Holy Spirit in helping him to remain faithful, the more he believed he could keep God's commandments to avoid fornication or adultery. He also began to desire to be faithful.

Apart from the Holy Spirit, a righteous life becomes legalistic and nearly impossible to maintain. With the help of the Holy Spirit, God's commandments can be kept until they become a heart's desire and the norm of one's life.

The apostle Paul addressed this very issue when he said –

> *Well then, am I suggesting that these laws of God are evil? Of course not! No, the law is not sinful, but it was the law that showed me my sin. I would never have known the sin in my heart – the evil desires that are hidden there – if the law had not said, "You must not have evil desires in your heart."*
>
> *But sin used this law against evil desires by reminding*

me that such desires are wrong, and arousing all kinds of forbidden desires within me! Only if there were no laws to break would there be no sinning.

That is why I felt fine so long as I did not understand what the law really demanded. But when I learned the truth, I realized that I had broken the law and was a sinner, doomed to die.

So as far as I was concerned, the good law which was supposed to show me the way of life resulted instead in my being given the death penalty

Romans 7:7–10 (TLB)

The law of God was not designed to make us right with God, but to show us our need for Him and for His help on a daily basis to remain in right relationship. A person who thinks that they can maintain control of their lives, always do the right things, or achieve a good relationship apart from God is a person who ultimately is denying the *need* for the Holy Spirit at work in his or her life. The commandments of God – and our inability to keep them – is a constant reminder to us that we need the presence of God working in us to *help* us do what it is that God desires for us to do, think, and say.

The more we are aware of our need for God, the more we should avail ourselves of His help. None of us is in a position to claim, "Well, I have a good marriage and I have had a good marriage for many years, so I can probably trust God less in this area." No! The need is to trust Him even more.

An Ongoing Need to Trust God for Relationship

The enemy of our souls and our marriages does not only prey

upon failing or weak marriages. Why bother? He already has a victory in those areas. The marriages the devil assaults are the strong marriages. To topple a strong marriage is a much greater coup for the devil than to destroy one that is already foundering.

Helen and Bert had what all of their friends perceived to be a very happy and fulfilling marriage. They had three grown children, a paid-up mortgage, and a longstanding relationship with many friends at their church. Bert, at age fifty, was already contemplating an early retirement and Helen was involved in activities that she found both rewarding and helpful to others.

The entire church community was in shock at the news that Helen and Bert had "separated." Nobody could imagine what had driven apart this seemingly perfect couple.

In truth, no one thing had caused the breakdown in their marriage. They both came to the same realization during a marriage counseling session: They had become too busy for each other and had simply drifted apart. Bert had allowed his work responsibilities and church committee memberships to absorb all of his time; any "free time" he had he spent playing golf with work buddies or church pastors (both of which he justified as being very important to his church and work relationships).

Helen hadn't really minded. She was equally absorbed in her volunteer work for various causes, and with caring part-time for their two-year-old grandchild.

When Bert and Helen slowed down enough to face their lives, they realized that they had little to converse about, little to which they could point as mutual interests, and therefore, they saw little reason to continue what had seemed to become a "hollow shell" of a marriage.

Fortunately, their children and friends raised such a protest at their separation that they sought out a Christian counselor to see if there was any hope at renewing their marriage. The counselor wisely pointed out to them that their "busy-ness" – including their many activities that supposedly were "for God" – had been the trick which the enemy had used against them. Nothing had gone wrong – rather, the enemy had used the tactic of "too much of the right things" to drive a wedge between them. The counselor refocused their attention on some basics: the children and grandchildren that they had in common, their many years of good memories and affection, their common faith. He encouraged them to begin dating again and to take time for meaningful conversations. He also encouraged them to start praying together again, and even to attend a spiritual retreat together.

Both Helen and Bert resigned from all of their volunteer activities to concentrate their time and energy on their marriage. And within several months, they had renewed their marriage vows and were living together again. They continued to work on their mutual tendencies to overbook their schedules. They made a weekly "date" a priority and they started attending a Bible study fellowship together on Wednesday nights. They refused to participate, however, in committee and other volunteer outreaches unless both of them could work together in the ministry.

Never assume that you have become too spiritually mature, or that you have been married "too long" to have marital difficulties. Continue to trust God daily for your marriage and to thank Him for giving you the spouse He has given you. It is true for you marriage, but also for every other area of your life:

We never outgrow our need for humble faith in God.

Continue to trust God for your covenant relationships today – both your relationship with God the Father as your Creator, Christ as your Savior, and the Holy Spirit as your Counselor . . . and your relationship with your spouse and other family members. God is your ever-present ally in helping you build strong relationships that can last a lifetime.

SCRIPTURES THAT CONFIRM:

God Is in Relationship with His People

There shall not any man be able to stand before thee all the days of thy life: as I was with Moses, so I will be with thee: I will not fail thee, nor forsake thee.

Be strong and of a good courage: for unto this people shalt thou divide for an inheritance the land, which I sware unto their fathers to give them.

Only be thou strong and very courageous, that thou mayest observe to do according to all the law, which Moses my servant commanded thee: turn not from it to the right hand or to the left, that thou mayest prosper whithersoever thou goest.

This book of the law shall not depart out of thy mouth; but thou shalt meditate therein day and night, that thou mayest observe to do according to all that is written therein: for then thou shalt make thy way prosperous, and then thou shalt have good success

Joshua 1:5–8

But let him who boasts boast about this: that he understands and knows me, that I am the Lord

Jeremiah 9:24 (NIV)

For as many as are led by the Spirit of God, they are the sons of God.

For ye have not received the spirit of bondage again to fear; but ye have received the Spirit of adoption, whereby we cry, Abba, Father.

The Spirit itself beareth witness with our spirit, that we are the children of God:

and if children, then heirs; heirs of God, and joint-heirs with Christ; if so be that we suffer with him, that we may be also glorified together.

For I reckon that the sufferings of this present time are not worthy to be compared with the glory which shall be revealed in us.

For the earnest expectation of the creature waiteth for the manifestation of the sons of God

Romans 8:14-19

CHAPTER 9

Chapter 9

Keeping Covenant Requires Faith

We each enter a covenant relationship *by faith*. And it is by faith that we live out our covenant relationships.

No relationship ever has a firm guarantee other than the relationship we have with Christ Jesus. In Him, the guarantee is certain: He will never leave nor forsake us. He will remain true, faithful, and loyal to us for the rest of our lives and on into eternity. He will always be there for us. Nothing can separate us from His love.

Our covenant relationship with our spouse *ideally* and before God has this same characteristic: an abiding and steadfast faithfulness. At the same time, we must recognize that as human beings, we make mistakes, we sin, we err unknowingly.

When one or both persons in the marriage relationship does sin, however, we must not be quick to say, "Well, that's that – end of marriage." Rather, we need to take the stance, "I choose to remain loyal to my spouse. There but for the grace of God go I."

You may not think that you are capable of the sin that your spouse has committed. You may not believe that you have as many flaws or failures as your spouse. In reality before God, you are just as much in need of God's grace as your spouse. It is not your "perfection" that keeps you in right relationship with God, and neither is it your "perfection" that will keep your marriage together or make it healthy. Rather, it is the grace of God to forgive, and the grace of one spouse to forgive another.

The power that holds us in covenant is not "works," but faith.

Give God Some "Credit"

Faith is a confidence that God is reliable. Hebrews 11:1 says, "Now faith is the substance of things hoped for, the evidence of things not seen." Some people read this verse and ask, "How can it be faith if there is substance and evidence involved?" Easy – the substance of all that we hope for, and the evidence that we will receive all that we hope for, lies in Jesus Christ. He is the substance. His reliability, His trustworthiness, His loyalty to us is all the evidence we need. *In* Him and *by* Him are all the things that we require.

The Latin root of the phrase "to believe" is the same root as the word "credit." When we exercise faith in God, we are doing exactly what the bank does for us when it gives us credit. We give God "credit," based on His history, His name, and His ability. We believe that He will provide what we need in faithfulness to His own promises. Faith is giving God credit that He is more than able to do what He says He will do.

The Bible reminds us repeatedly that God certainly has a good credit history. In Hebrews 11:3 we read, "Through faith we understand that the worlds were framed by the word of God, so that things which are seen were not made of things which do appear."

The fact is, God has a solution for any problem that may arise in your marriage. That solution may at present lie in the unseen realm of the spirit. When we exercise our faith in God, we are saying, in effect, "God, I know You have a way through this difficulty or problem. And I know I can trust You to act and to bring us through this hard time." This is saying not only that you believe God can act on your behalf, but that He *will* act for your good.

God's Desires for You

Hebrews 11:5-6 reminds us that God is a "rewarder" of those who have faith in Him. In other words, He doesn't disappoint those who come to Him in faith, but rather, He "rewards" them with blessings –

> *By faith Enoch was translated that he should not see death; and was not found, because God had translated him: for before his translation he had this testimony, that he pleased God.*
>
> *But without faith it is impossible to please him: for he that cometh to God must believe that he is, and that he is a rewarder of them that diligently seek him.*

God desires that we come to Him, asking boldly for those things that will be a blessing to us and to our families. In asking things of Him with faith, we are giving God the privilege of overriding our free will and of establishing His will. We do so believing that God's will for us is good – that He will give us precisely what we need for living the most abundant life possible, and ultimately, an eternal life with Him.

Hebrews 11 lists a number of "superstars" of the Bible. What marks them as superstars is that they all "judged Him faithful who had promised."

Note that phrase, "who had promised." If we approach God and ask Him for something that He has not promised, we have a faith that is ill-founded or misplaced. When that happens, we are not truly asking in faith, but out of presumption. We are asking for what we want, without regard to what it is that God has promised to us. We must be very sure that when we ask God to do things in our lives or the lives of those we love, we are asking Him for things that He has already stated in His Word that He desires for us to have.

What are some of the things that God has made very clear in His Word that He desires for us? Here are just a few of His promised blessings –

• **Health** – not only in our bodies, but in our minds, emotions, spirits, finances, and relationships. In 3 John 2 we read, "Beloved, I wish above all things that thou mayest prosper and be in health, even as thy soul prospereth." The Bible has miracles of healing, deliverance, and salvation from cover to cover!

• **Deliverance from Evil** – and an ability to confront and to overcome the enemy of our souls. In 1 John 4:4 we have God's promise, "Greater is he [the Holy Spirit] that is in you, than he [the devil] that is in the world."

• **Love.** In 1 John 4:11 we read, "Beloved, if God so loved us, we ought also to love one another."

• **Freedom from Fear.** We are not to be bound up in fears that are born of jealousy, threats, or persecution. In 1 John 4:18 we read that "Perfect love casteth out fear."

• **Emotional Stability.** God's choice for us is that we have relationships that are marked by stability, reason, affection. In 2 Timothy 1:7 we read, "God hath not given us the spirit of fear; but of power, and of love, and of a sound mind."

• **Wisdom.** God does not desire that we live in confusion or that we be bound by problems or needs. Rather, He desires to give us His wisdom so we will know what to do, how to act, when to take action, what to say, and which choices to make. James 1:5–6 encourages us, "If any of you lack wisdom, let him ask of God, that giveth to all men liberally, and upbraideth not; and it shall be given him, but let him ask in faith, nothing wavering."

You can go to God at any time and ask in *faith* for God to supply you, or others in your family, with any of these blessings. God will be faithful to supply what you need because He has already promised you that these blessings are available to you!

Many people spend far more time asking God for material and tangible things than they do the things that are listed above. It is sobering to think that far more prayers are voiced for new jobs, new cars, and new houses than are ever voiced for "more wisdom."

We certainly aren't saying that God is *not* concerned about our having the material and tangible goods and services that we need. The Bible, however, makes it clear that our priority is to be on acquiring and developing spiritual traits. Jesus taught –

> *Take no thought for your life, what ye shall eat, or what ye shall drink; nor yet for your body, what ye shall put on. Is not the life more than meat, and the body than raiment?...*
>
> *But seek ye first the kingdom of God, and his righteousness; and all these things shall be added unto you*
>
> Matthew 6:25, 33

Stop to think for a moment about what a wonderful marriage you would have if at all times you and your spouse were experiencing wholeness in spirit, mind, and body (wholeness being the ultimate in good health!); deliverance from evil (including evil temptations); love that is free-flowing and unconditional; freedom from fear; emotional stability; and the wisdom of God. There simply wouldn't be a problem that you could not overcome, endure, or resolve! These are all things that God *desires* for you to experience, and to claim as being part of your life and your marriage *by faith.*

Furthermore, if you and your spouse are overflowing with health (which includes energy) and love and wisdom . . . you will know what it is that you are to do in order to *have* the material and tangible things that you need and desire for your family. God will pour out upon you the ideas and opportunities you need in order to prosper fully.

Putting God's Desires First

Our challenge as self-centered human beings is to put what God desires before our own desires. Those who truly live by faith are not people who major on their past failures or on their fleshly desires. Instead, they major on God and what He can and will do.

The Bible has a wonderful story about the benefits of putting God first and then reaping tangible rewards later. It is the story of Abraham and Lot, found in Genesis 13-15. Abraham and Lot, Abraham's nephew, were so blessed in the growth of their flocks and herds that eventually, there was not enough foliage to feed all of the animals. They decided to separate. Abraham gave Lot his choice of land and Lot chose the fertile plains. Abraham chose to trust God in this, however, and moved into the less desirable land.

What happened to Abraham as the result of His trusting God in this matter and of putting God's will first? He received this prophecy from the Lord –

> *And the Lord said unto Abram, after that Lot was separated from him, Lift up now thine eyes, and look from the place where thou art northward, and southward, and eastward, and westward:*
>
> *For all the land which thou seest, to thee will I give it, and to thy seed for ever.*
>
> *And I will make thy seed as the dust of the earth: so that if a man can number the dust of the earth, then shall thy*

seed also be numbered

Genesis 13:14–16

In putting God first, Abraham received all of the land he could see, and not only for himself, but his heirs. That land was later described in Genesis 15:18–21 (NIV) as all of the land "from the river of Egypt to the great river, the Euphrates – the land of the Kenites, Kenizzites, Kadmonites, Hittites, Perizzites, Rephaites, Amorites, Canaanites, Girgashites and Jebusites."

Lot, who had made his choice out of his own desire and wisdom, received a land that at first seemed the better land, but which later was destroyed to a great extent by the punishment brought upon Sodom and Gomorrah.

Jesus promised clearly, "If you cling to your life, you will lose it; but if you give it up for me, you will save it" (Matthew 10:39 TLB).

Ask God to Increase Your Faith for Your Marriage

We each will get to heaven *by faith.* Ephesians 2:8–9 spells it out clearly, "For by grace are ye saved through faith; and that not of yourselves: it is the gift of God: not of works, lest any man should boast."

If we are to experience a little bit of heaven on earth in our marriages, we are also going to experience them *by faith.*

Notice what Paul said in Ephesians regarding our faith – it is a "gift of God." What an important truth this is for us to grasp! Faith is not something we "work up" or "create." It is a gift of God to us. We each have been given a measure of faith, and it is up to us to develop that faith. When we ask God to increase our faith, however, we can be assured that He will do so. God's desire is that we grow in our faith until we have *great faith.*

Lucy found herself utterly devastated when her husband told her that he was leaving her for a younger woman. Lucy was a beautiful woman, married to Victor for twenty years. They had three children, a lovely home, a cat, and a dog. She had seemed to have the perfect life.

As the weeks went by and divorce seemed to loom before her, Lucy felt increasing hurt and shame, and in response to those emotions, she also became increasingly angry at what Vic was "throwing away." She found herself saying repeatedly, *How can he do this to me and the children? How can he walk away after we have shared and enjoyed so many years together?*

Lucy became so angry that she eventually didn't even want Victor to return. *How could I ever trust him again?* she replied to friends who told her that they were praying and believing for reconciliation.

Finally one of Lucy's friends said to her, "Lucy, your friends are all praying that Victor will come to his senses and return to you and the kids, but you've got to want him back!"

In tears, Lucy said, "But I don't want him back."

Her friend replied to her in truth, although she spoke it with a great deal of compassion, "Then you are just as much in error as Vic."

Lucy reacted. "What do you mean, just as much in error? I'm not running off with another man. I'm not the one filing for divorce."

"But your anger is just as wrong before God as Vic's dating another woman," the friend said.

Lucy was stunned. She had never considered that possibility. In fact, she had never considered the possibility that she had done *anything* wrong in their marriage.

Lucy sought out a Christian counselor to help her deal with the pain that she felt at this rebuke from her friend. In counseling sessions, she began to see areas in which she had made some serious mistakes in her relationship with Vic. She began to work on those areas of her life. She also confessed her anger and growing hatred and bitterness as sins before God. As part of her prayer for forgiveness, Lucy prayed, "Lord, help me to forgive Vic. I don't really want to forgive him but I know I need to forgive him. Help me to *want* to forgive him. In fact, help me to *want to WANT TO* forgive him."

The Lord heard and answered Lucy's prayer. In the days that followed, she felt a new freedom and peace in her heart. She felt a release in her emotions regarding Vic. When she met with Vic and their attorneys the next time – which was about three weeks later – Vic could see the change in her. He confided to a friend, "She had a glow on her face I had never seen. She genuinely seemed happy. I was curious to find out why."

They talked together after the session with their attorneys that day and as part of their conversation, Lucy asked Vic to forgive her for the mistakes she had made in their marriage. She told him about her experience of forgiveness from God and about the growing desire she had felt in her heart that she needed also to ask for forgiveness from Vic.

Vic was stunned by her admission that she had failed in some ways in their marriage. He found himself forgiving Lucy and then, asking for *her* forgiveness. At that point, Lucy was ready to forgive. Her heart seemed to be softened and healed even more during that hour with Vic.

In the following weeks, Lucy and Vic talked several times on the phone and then one night, Vic called to invite Lucy to dinner. They had a good time together and began to see each other more regularly. Vic broke off his relationship with the other woman, and eventually, Vic agreed to see Lucy's counselor with her, as well as separately.

What had seemed like a perfect marriage to Lucy had, in fact, been a marriage with some serious flaws. The Christian counselor helped them work on a number of areas in which they both needed healing, better communication skills, and a greater understanding.

Although it took more than a year, Vic and Lucy eventually were reunited and their marriage vows were renewed. They have been married three years now and still see a counselor periodically, but they have come to a new realization that marriage not only is something that both parties must *work* at, but something which both partners need to *believe* for.

Marriage is a walk of faith just as the rest of a person's Christian life is a walk of faith.

Build Up Your Faith!

If you are feeling low in your faith, choose to read some of the great faith-building passages in God's Word. Here are eight suggestions – in many cases, these stories can be applied to your relationships. For example, in reading about Noah, you might look for ways in which God is calling you to trust Him even through a flood of difficulty. In reading about Jesus' healing of a paralytic, you might look for insight into how God heals us and uses friends as part of the process when we are "too scared to move."

As you read these passages, write down in the margins of your Bible the applications you see to your own life and marriage:

· Genesis 6:14–22 (Noah building the ark)
· Genesis 12:1–4 (Abraham leaving for a land God has said He will show him)
· Exodus 14 and 15 (Moses and the children of Israel at the Red Sea)
· Numbers 14:6–9 (Joshua and Caleb believing that the Israelites can "take" the land)
· Judges 6:36–40 and 7 (Gideon)
· Daniel 6:4-23 (Daniel forbidden to pray)
· Matthew 9:18,23–25 (Jesus raising daughter of Jairus from death)
· Luke 5:18–20 (Friends bringing paralyzed man to Jesus for healing)

Ask God in Faith

Because of your acceptance of Jesus Christ as Savior, you have been given open access to the throne room of God. There, you can ask for anything that you desire *in the name of Jesus.* You have been given access to power and strength far beyond that which you have in yourself. You are tied to the unlimited power of Christ!

What is it that you are requesting of God for your personal life? For your marriage? Come to the Lord in faith and request it!

A great and good outcome belongs to those who are faithful saints of God. As Hebrews 11:33–34 tells us –

> *Who through faith subdued kingdoms, wrought righteousness, obtained promises [all the promises, which includes reconciliation of hearts], stopped the mouths of lions,*
>
> *quenched the violence of fire, escaped the edge of the sword, out of weakness were made strong, waxed valiant in fight, turned to flight the armies of the aliens [to*

include the ones who may have invaded your matrimonial land].

Those who understand the power of the covenant, and unleash its power through their faith, are in a position to see a great victory in their lives! Believe God for the very best your marriage can be.

Scriptures That Confirm:

We Are Called by God to Walk by Faith

Seek not ye what ye shall eat, or what ye shall drink, neither be ye of doubtful mind.

For all these things do the nations of the world seek after: and your Father knoweth that ye have need of these things.

But rather seek ye the kingdom of God; and all these things shall be added unto you

Luke 12:29–31

We walk by faith, not by sight

2 Corinthians 5:7

For ye have need of patience, that, after ye have done the will of God, ye might receive the promise.

For yet a little while, and he that shall come will come, and will not tarry. Now the just shall live by faith; but if any man draw back, my soul shall have no pleasure in him

Hebrews 10:36–38

Without faith it is impossible to please him

Hebrews 11:6

Chapter 10

Chapter 10

Freely Giving and Forgiving

How much healing, restoration, and growth would occur in marriages if each person would only deal generously and lovingly toward their spouse *regardless of what the spouse did or said!*

As Christians we very often err when we think that one type of sin is "worse" than another. According to the Law of Moses, all sins and transgressions against the Law are equally destructive. Sin is sin, regardless of its nature, quantity, or magnitude. That is why we are more accurate to refer to our "sin nature" rather than to individual sinful acts. From God's perspective, for example, the sins of murder and gossip are equal!

Since this is the case, there is simply no way that any person can ever claim to have lived a sin-free life. We all have, are, or will break the Law. As Paul said, "All have sinned, and come short of the glory of God" (Romans 3:23).

Even so, because God has established a covenant with us through Christ Jesus, He continues to love us even though we commit sins from time to time, sometimes willfully and sometimes in ignorance. We come to Him by faith initially to receive His forgiveness for our sin nature, and then we continue to come to Christ daily to receive a cleansing of forgiveness for our daily sinful deeds. The covenant is established by faith, and it is continually renewed by faith.

An important truth for you to recognize about your marriage is that you entered it *by faith*. You trusted that you would be able to have a good marriage.

And no matter what kind of marriage you find yourself in, your covenant relationship with your spouse is subject to the same criterion of sin that pertains to your covenant relationship with God – all sins are equally devastating from God's viewpoint. This means, for example, that lying about why you were late in coming home is just as much a sin in God's eyes as having a sexual relationship with someone other than your spouse!

It would seem, therefore, that we are all doomed to failure! Nobody can be perfect before God and nobody can be perfect in a relationship with another person. We each will sin in our marriage relationships – sometimes our sins may seem to be minor, sometimes major, sometimes committed by an act of the will, sometimes by carelessness or even unknowingly.

How must we respond? In the same way Christ loves us. He forgives us, and He calls us to forgive others. We each are called to walk *by faith* in our marriages – not solely to enter our marriages by faith but to continue to walk out our married life by faith.

Forgiveness is the key to a renewal of our faith – it is vital in both our relationship with God and our relationship with our spouse.

The Overflow of a Generous Heart

One of the most powerful stories in the Bible about covenant involves Mephibosheth, a son of Jonathan and grandson of King Saul. (This story is found in 1 Samuel 18-19 and 2 Samuel 9.)

Apart from Mephibosheth, there are three main characters in this story:

· King Saul – a man whom God chose to be king, but who soon lost his humility and always seemed to have a "better idea" than God about how to live as king.

· David – a man "after God's own heart" who loved God and sought the will of God.

· Jonathan – a man caught between Saul, his father, and David, his friend.

Jonathan and David entered into a covenant relationship, which is described in 1 Samuel 18:1-4 (TLB) –

> *After King Saul had finished his conversation with David, David met Jonathan, the king's son, and there was an immediate bond of love between them. Jonathan swore to be his blood brother, and sealed the pact by giving him his robe, sword, bow, and belt.*
>
> *King Saul now kept David at Jerusalem and wouldn't let him return home any more.*

The relationship between King Saul and David was a stormy one, rising from King Saul's jealousy of David. Saul ultimately forced David to flee for his life and he did so, with the help of his covenant friend Jonathan.

A number of years later, Saul's rebellion resulted in Saul being killed in a battle. Jonathan died on the same day in the same conflict. When word came back to Saul's home that both Saul and Jonathan had been killed, the nurse responsible for the care of young Mephibosheth, who was five years old at the time, scooped him up and attempted to flee with him. She clumsily dropped Mephibosheth in her haste and the result was that the boy grew up lame in both legs.

The custom in those days was for a rising king to seek out all members of the defeated king's family and kill them so they might make no claim to the throne. No doubt Mephibosheth grew up in terror that David might one day find him. What he likely didn't know was that David and his father Jonathan were in a blood covenant.

In mourning for his covenant friend, David began to ask about any heirs of Jonathan who might still be alive. His search led him to Mephibosheth. In 2 Samuel 9:5-7 (TLB) we read –

> *So King David sent for Mephibosheth – Jonathan's son and Saul's grandson.*
>
> *Mephibosheth arrived in great fear and greeted the king in deep humility, bowing low before him,*
>
> *but David said, "Don't be afraid! I've asked you to come so that I can be kind to you because of my vow to your father Jonathan. I will restore to you all the land of your grandfather Saul, and you shall live here at the palace!"*

The words of King David no doubt seemed incredulous to Mephibosheth. In 2 Samuel 9:8 (TLB) we read his response: "Mephibosheth fell to the ground before the king and exclaimed, 'Should the king show kindness to a dead dog like me?'" Mephibosheth had not supported or helped David, and he had little reason to expect such kindness from the man his grandfather had considered to be such an arch enemy. It surely was almost beyond his imagination to think that David would extend such a generous invitation to him.

The Bible does not give us the details but we might guess at them – that perhaps David got down off the throne and walked over to Mephibosheth and said, "This has nothing to do with your worth or your deeds. See this scar on my wrist? I cut covenant with your father Jonathan and you are a part of it as his son. Go look in my closet and you can see the robe and sword your father gave me as a part of our covenant."

For his part, Mephibosheth did not let bitterness, anger, distrust, or hatred enter his heart. He took David up on his offer and moved into the palace. He probably didn't take long to conclude, *I'm glad to have lands and titles again. And what a luxury to live in a palace and be waited upon by servants as if I am a prince.*

Mephibosheth didn't have any "right" politically, socially, or legally to what David gave to him. David's generosity of spirit flowed from his love for Jonathan and his covenant relationship with Jonathan.

We err greatly any time we conclude that we have a "right" to God's blessings or that God in some way is indebted to us. To the contrary, we are indebted to Him! Everything we have flows from God's love for us and the covenant relationship He has established with us through Jesus Christ, His Son.

Like Mephibosheth, we are recipients of God's beneficial grace and mercy extended to us. All of Christ's Kingdom is made available to us. We are blessed with the rewards of the inheritance that has been given by the Father to Jesus. We are "joint heirs" with Him. Just as the Father freely gave all of Himself to Jesus, so Jesus freely gives all of Himself to us.

What a wonderful image of generosity this is for us to hold before us as we live in a marriage relationship. As the Lord has been so generous to us, so we must be generous to our spouse.

Linda decided to address this issue in a very practical and persistent way in her marriage. Her husband Ron was often critical of her — putting her down before their children and others, nearly always without any apparent cause or justification. Linda chose to respond to his critical comments with exactly what Ron *didn't* deserve – praise and appreciation!

When Ron would say, "That's a terrible looking dress," Linda would respond very sweetly and without any sarcasm, "Thank you for telling me that. I appreciate your good judgment. Perhaps next time I go dress shopping, you can come along and help me make a better choice." If Ron criticized a meal she prepared, Linda said in an upbeat way, "It helps me to know what you don't like, Ron, so I won't prepare this again."

Several things happened. Ron found it very little fun to criticize a wife who wouldn't "fight back." Linda had the satisfaction of knowing that she was being a good example to her children of turning the other cheek and of responding in kindness and love, regardless of Ron's behavior. And eventually, Ron saw that his criticism was getting nowhere and his negative comments became fewer and fewer. Once Ron turned away from the negative, he found it much easier to be more positive!

We Never "Deserve" or Earn God's Blessing

The fact is, no spouse will ever "deserve" what he or she "desires" in the way of blessings. And neither will you as a spouse! We must have a clear understanding about this. God's mercy and love flow from God's heart. They are never extended to us on the basis of our worthiness. We are to be like God in the mercy and love we give to our spouse.

Anytime we ask a spouse to "earn" our love or to be "worthy" of our love, we have moved to a position of conditional love rather than unconditional love. That is not God's nature, not God's plan, not the work of the Holy Spirit, and not what is pleasing to God. It also is a position that will be very unsatisfying to both you and your spouse, and which will build resentment and distrust in your marriage!

Our desire must be to rise above all expectations and scorekeeping in our marriages and give to one another with generous hearts.

For years, Wanda kept score. When Sam won an argument, she chalked it up as "one for Sam." When she felt that she had won an argument or had her say in a decision, she countered with "one for Wanda."

If Sam got a night out, Wanda demanded a night out. If Sam spent twenty dollars on a special item for his personal use, Wanda spent twenty dollars on an item just for herself. Wanda didn't necessarily "compete" with Sam, she just made sure that she got equal time, equal resources, and equal attention.

In one area, Wanda's scorekeeping got a little lopsided. She remembered *all* of Sam's sins, but hardly any of her own.

During a revival meeting at her church, Wanda came face to face with her scorekeeping. God had freely forgiven her and loved her with generously. Wanda realized that she must forgive in like manner and develop a generous heart toward others, and especially toward her husband Sam.

What a difference her change of heart made in her marriage! Sam felt as if he was let out of a cage. And Wanda actually felt the same way. She no longer needed to keep tabs on all that Sam did, said, or spent.

Wanda began to have fun planning special surprises and treats for Sam. And the more she did so, the more she discovered that Sam was treating her more special and actually spending more time, energy, and money on her than he had in the past. She discovered that it truly was more "fun" to give than to receive.

Giving Freely and Out of Love

To give freely and unconditionally out of love and mercy means that

- You praise your spouse for what he or she has done – without expecting praise in return.
- You seek the best for your spouse – regardless of his or her past behavior.
- You build up and encourage the good character qualities of your spouse – without mention of your spouse's faults.
- You choose to do loving and generous acts of kindness for your spouse – regardless of your spouse's mood or whether your spouse is appreciative of what you do.

What happens when you treat a spouse this way?

Two things. First, your spouse eventually will respond to your love. It may take time, but the response will come.

Second, and perhaps more importantly, your own heart will soften. Any hard "rocks" of bitterness, anger, and resentment that you have in your heart will soften. You will have a greater feeling of freedom in your own spirit.

The Key to Genuine Forgiveness. It is out of this spirit of unconditional love and generous giving that a person begins to feel genuine forgiveness.

We each know how wonderful we felt when we first experienced the unconditional love of God and God's full forgiveness of our sin nature! We felt clean, valuable, free, and at peace.

In a marriage relationship, when your spouse truly *feels* your unconditional love and forgiveness, your spouse will also feel more valuable, free, and at peace. A "settled-ness" will enter your spouse's heart in response to you.

Now, if your spouse does not know the Lord Jesus Christ as Savior, then your spouse is also likely to feel greater conviction to receive Christ into his life. Your spouse is likely to have a greater desire to feel the full forgiveness of God.

The result of love and forgiveness, however, is always – ultimately – one of inner joy, peace, and esteem.

And what happens to you, the one who is forgiving and loving? First, you are in a greater position to be forgiven by God yourself. Luke 6:37 tells us, "Judge not, and ye shall not be judged: condemn not, and ye shall not be condemned: forgive, and ye shall be forgiven." In Matthew 6:14–15 we read, "For if ye forgive men their trespasses, your heavenly Father will also forgive you: but if ye forgive not men their trespasses, neither will your Father forgive your trespasses."

Second, the more you give love to others, the more you will experience God's love and the love of others in return. You simply cannot outgive God, and you cannot outlove God. What love you give, you will receive – and then some. Our giving is always multiplied back to us in the very form we need most. Our acts of kindness and love come back to us in amounts that are generous, abundant, and at times, overwhelming.

Love generously.
Give generously.
Forgive generously.

You'll see a change in your spouse, and also experience a change in your own soul. You likely will find that you have a more loving, generous, and forgiving spouse. You most certainly will find that you are becoming a more loving, generous, and forgiving person!

Liz heard this teaching about generous giving and forgiveness and decided to give it a try. She and Rob had been having a difficult time in their marriage and much of it Liz blamed on Rob's selfish attitude. She had felt that to give to Rob was simply to bolster his insatiable desire to accumulate and control.

Liz began to tuck little love notes in lunches that she thoughtfully prepared for Rob. She left a red rose in his bathroom with a little note, "I love you." She made sure she folded the newspaper just the way Rob liked it folded after she had read it. She made his favorite foods for dinner. She responded with kind words, even during his angry outbursts.

At first Rob didn't even seem to notice all of Liz's giving, but eventually he did. And to Liz's great amazement, he began to give back! Liz found she enjoyed giving and receiving much more than hoarding, criticizing, and nagging!

Continual, Consistent Giving. Throughout the Scripture we find many admonitions to remain steadfast in faith. The same is true for our giving. David did not invite Mephibosheth to the palace for one meal. He did not give him back his lands for just one harvest season. Our generosity of spirit must not be limited to one occasion, one act, one encounter. We must be continual and consistent in our giving just as we remain steadfast and consistent in our faith.

Neither should we lose patience in our giving and believing when we see no progress. God is never in a "hurry." He does things according to a sovereign timetable with a backdrop of all eternity. We should never engage in a loving act of service, or a generous act of giving, and then immediately expect God to turn everything around in the direction we desire. God sees the beginning from the ending. He knows each person who is involved and He is about a greater work at all times – to bring us into wholeness and to "grow us up" into the likeness of Jesus Christ.

Giving and Faith Are Processes. The Scriptures tell us that we "grow" in grace, in faith, and in our capacity for giving. We are to be in a state of developing a larger and larger heart toward both God and others. We are to receive more and more from God, believe for more and more, and give more and more.

Those who receive from us are also in process. When we expect an "immediate return" on our giving, we err. God will use our giving as a part of His ongoing process in the person's life.

Alice was very upset when she made a wonderful, candlelit, homemade, four-course dinner for her husband, only to have him eat it, yawn, and move immediately to his easy chair in the living room where he fell asleep. She felt shortchanged. Why hadn't he responded with more affection and appreciation? She began to question, *Did God care?*

What Alice could not see was that her act of kindness to her husband was like a foundation stone set for a new pattern in her relationship with her husband. It was not a magic cure-all, but a *step* in the right direction of giving to her husband. In not criticizing her husband for failing to appreciate her effort more, she added another foundation stone.

But in harboring anger and resentment in her own heart, she negated some of what she had done – not in her husband's life but in her own! Her better tactic would have been to cover up her husband with a blanket and tuck a pillow under his head in his easy chair.

A one-time event is not going to work miracles in any relationship. But every act of giving is going to count in the overall process of healing, restoration, and of building up a relationship in God's overall plan for wholeness.

Jesus told a parable about two people who built houses. One

built on sand and when the rain fell, the winds blew, and the flood waters rose, the house collapsed. The other built on a solid rock and when the storm hit, the house survived "for it was founded upon a rock" (Matthew 7:25). The process of continuing to give to a spouse with love and in faith is the process of building upon a rock. A house is not built in a day, and especially a house that is established on the firm bedrock of Christ's words. Love and faith must be expressed day after day . . . after day after day . . . after day after day. It is the daily expression of love and faith that creates a sure foundation.

This is not to say that God cannot work His miracles quickly. There are times when a single act of giving or kindness seems to have an immediate impact. The likely probability, however, is that this single act is part of a long string of actions or that it is the action that is a culmination of a growing faith.

For example, a woman touched the hem of Jesus' garment and was made whole immediately. But this came after a certain progression of her faith that occurred when she made the bold decision to go to Jesus, and then to move through a crowd to get to Him. With each step, each move past another person in that crowd, her faith built.

A Roman centurion who asked Jesus to heal his servant was rewarded with an immediate response, but this was also part of a progression that is not fully described in the Scriptures. This centurion had already shown love and compassion for his servant by taking care of him during his sickness. He had made the effort of faith to dispatch someone to Jesus. He was believing for the healing of his servant long before the messenger arrived at the place where Jesus was ministering, and long before the messenger returned home to the centurion.

Our part is to establish an ongoing pattern of giving and to build up our faith, step by step. We must leave the decision totally in God's hands as to *when* and *how* He will bring a miracle to pass in our lives and in our marriage.

Faith Is the Key to God's Power

From the beginning, Satan had both a desire and a plan to steal man's personal relationship with God. God's desire has been even more ardent and his plan even more profound for restoring a personal relationship with man. That plan for restoration is rooted in the concept of covenant. Regardless of circumstances, God's covenant plan remains firm.

The same covenant power that restores man to God, and which seals man's relationship with his Heavenly Father, is the power available to men and women who enter a marriage relationship. Regardless of circumstances, God's covenant prevails!

Because this is true, we can persist in faith, knowing that God is about redemption and perfection at all times – our redemption and perfection as well as that of our spouse.

How can you give to a person who is undeserving, and who in your opinion may be "unworthy" of your love, affection, or generosity? Only by faith!

When we give to someone who has wronged us, hurt us, rejected us, or maligned us, we are to do so with an attitude of faith toward God. We give and our prayer as we do is this: "Father, let this gift come as if from You to this person. Let it be an expression of Your love for this person. Let it accomplish what You desire in this person's life, which is a renewed relationship with You."

To give out of a sense of changing a person is to have a manipulative spirit born of human will and desire. To give out of a genuine sense of mercy and love – with no regard to any outcome other than to give freely as Christ has given to us – is to have a heart of faith and mercy.

The good news is that when we give to a person out of genuine unconditional love – expecting nothing in return from the person but expecting God to do great things in and for the person – we will see miracles. Faith does not return void. God honors our faith and responds to it. He is a rewarder of those who operate in faith and who give in love.

• **We Are Made Whole.** In some cases, the miracle that comes to us is our own healing of hurt, anger, or rejection.

For several months, Inez and Carla met to pray for their husbands. They had felt deeply wounded and rejected by their spouses although both were still married. They both desired better marriages.

Inez had been taught at her church to pray for very specific things and she shared this teaching with Carla. Together, they began to meet weekly to pray for the "details" related to the putdowns and emotional hurts they had felt.

Although Inez and Carla could point to very few things that changed in their husband's behavior during those months of prayer, they could point to changes *they* experienced in their own hearts. By praying for their husbands, each woman had received a personal emotional healing from the Lord. Inez felt much stronger in her worth and value to God. Carla felt much more loved by God.

Inez and Carla brought this newfound strength and wholeness to their marriages and their husbands slowly, but surely, responded to the "newness" they saw in their wives. They saw a strength they admired and many of the criticisms and "put-downs" stopped. They also saw a deeper faith, and both men found themselves highly attracted to this in their wives. They began to spend more time with their wives and to value them more.

· **Others Are Made Whole.** In other cases, the miracle is a change in the heart of the person to whom we have made our gift.

Todd couldn't imagine how God could ever touch the heart of his wife Ann. She seemed resolute on separating from him, with the full intent of seeking a divorce. Although he had tried repeatedly to understand what she found so "wrong" with their marriage, she refused to respond to him. She simply said she wanted out and wanted her freedom. She could offer no explanation for her change of heart.

Todd began to intercede for Ann. He prayed for everything from her childhood memories to the influence of some new friends she had made. He trusted God to cause yet another change in her heart so that she might desire to stay in their marriage.

One day Ann came to him out of the blue and said, "I've changed my mind. I'm not leaving." Her decision to stay was just as abrupt as her decision to leave, and furthermore, Ann had absolutely no explanation for this change either.

Todd did not question God about "how" God had worked this miracle in Ann's heart or in their marriage, but he certainly began to praise Him for it. And he continued to pray for Ann that she might be strengthened in her resolve regarding their marriage and no longer be led by a whim of emotions or the counsel of others. His daily prayer for Ann was an outpouring of his love and faith.

Regardless of Outcome . . .

Regardless of the outcome of our giving, however, we are to *continue* to give to others with generosity and as an act of our faith. It is only then that God truly has a platform on which to build us up and to make us whole.

The same holds true for our forgiving. When Jesus' apostles asked Him how many times they were to forgive, Jesus responded with a "play on numbers" – He said we are to forgive "seventy times seven" (Matthew 18:22). Since seven is the number that is a symbol for perfection in the Scriptures, and ten is the number related to the law and to increase, Jesus was saying, in effect, that the perfect law of God to bring increase into your life is that you forgive and forgive and forgive, without counting how many times! Our forgiving must come from a generous heart, one that is truly *overflowing* with God's love.

SCRIPTURES THAT CONFIRM:

We Are To Give Generously and Out of Our Steadfast Faith

Therefore thus saith the Lord God, Behold I lay in Zion for a foundation a stone, a tried stone, a precious corner stone, a sure foundation: he that believeth shall not make haste

Isaiah 28:16

Therefore whosoever heareth these sayings of mine, and doeth them, I will liken him unto a wise man, which built his house upon a rock:

and the rain descended, and the floods came, and the winds blew, and beat upon that house; and it fell not: for it was founded upon a rock

Matthew 7:24–25

Jesus said unto the centurion, Go thy way; and as thou hast believed, so be it done unto thee. And his servant was healed in the selfsame hour

Matthew 8:13

Jesus turned him about, and when he saw her, he said, Daughter, be of good comfort; thy faith hath made thee whole. And the woman was made whole from that hour

Matthew 9:22

Then touched he their eyes, saying, According to your faith be it unto you

Matthew 9:29

Peter answered him and said, Lord, if it be thou, bid me come unto thee on the water.

And he said, Come. And when Peter was come down out of the ship, he walked on the water, to go to Jesus.

But when he saw the wind boisterous, he was afraid; and beginning to sink, he cried, saying, Lord, save me!

Matthew 14:28–30

Then Jesus answered and said unto her, O woman, great is thy faith: be it unto thee even as thou wilt. And her daughter was made whole from that very hour

Matthew 15:28

Jesus said unto him, If thou canst believe, all things are possible to him that believeth

Mark 9:23

The Lord said, If ye had faith as a grain of mustard seed, ye might say unto this sycamine tree, Be thou plucked up by the root, and be thou planted in the sea; and it should obey you

Luke 17:6

But as many as received him, to them gave he power to become the sons of God, even to them that believe on his name

John 1:12

Jesus said unto them, I am the bread of life: he that cometh to me shall never hunger; and he that believeth on me shall never thirst

John 6:35

Believe me that I am in the Father, and the Father in me: or else believe me for the very works' sake.

Verily, verily, I say unto you, He that believeth on me, the works that I do shall he do also; and greater works than these shall he do; because I go unto my Father

John 14:11-12

Chapter 11

Chapter 11

Staying Encouraged During Difficult Times

Do not be surprised if you have hard times in your marriage or in your life. If anything, these times of "persecution" should be expected, because in the end, all people face times of suffering and difficulty.

As the apostle Peter teaches us in his first letter, however, we must be sure that we are persecuted for doing right, not for doing what is wrong in God's eyes. (See 1 Peter 3:17.) When we sin, we should not be surprised when we are persecuted or punished by society. When we sin and we are God's children, He will chastise us. We can count on that. The reason is that God does not desire for any of His children to continue in error, but rather, that they might change their ways and live in a way that is righteous, pure, and holy before Him.

Jesus told us that we should not be surprised if we are persecuted for taking a Christlike stand in any situation, circumstance, or time of trouble. He said –

> *And ye shall be hated of all men for my name's sake: but he that endureth to the end shall be saved*
>
> Matthew 10:22

Notice especially that phrase, "he that endureth to the end shall be saved." God calls us to take courage in times of persecution. We are to *endure* what happens to us without wavering in our love and trust of God. In the end, God will prove to be victorious in our lives.

Two Things to Remember During Difficult Times

When difficulties arise in your life, it is very important that you remember who you are in Christ Jesus. Throughout the Old Testament, we find a number of occasions when the Israelites brought to their remembrance God's Law or times past in which God had delivered them or provided for them. It is so easy to say when trouble strikes, "Where's God? Doesn't He love me anymore?" The answer is, "God is always present and YES, He loves you beyond measure."

Two of the most important things you should remember in crisis or hard times are:

- God has a plan for you, His beloved child.
- God is not surprised at what is happening in your life.

A Plan for His Beloved. You were born "equipped" for a special place in God's kingdom and a specific role to play. One of the most liberating truths that you can ever grasp is this: "You are not an accident but rather, a chosen vessel of God's love and favor."

Each of us is vitally important to God's plan. The prophet Jeremiah spoke these words of the Lord –

> *Before I formed thee in the belly I knew thee; and before thou camest forth out of the womb I sanctified thee, and I ordained thee a prophet unto the nations*
>
> Jeremiah 1:5

Whenever you face a trouble or trial in life, or in your marriage relationship, remember that God loves you. It is very easy to lose sight of this fact if someone you love is criticizing you or if you are facing a real attack from Satan in any area of your life. God's love for you is perfect and ongoing; you are one of His beloved children.

The Bible tells us –

Ye are a chosen generation, a royal priesthood, an holy nation, a peculiar people; that ye should shew forth the praises of him who hath called you out of darkness into his marvelous light

1 Peter 2:9

If others are putting you down, persecuting you, or causing you problems, remember that you are a "chosen child" of the Almighty and Everlasting God.

God Is Not Surprised. It is impossible to surprise God. He sees everything and knows everything.

Paul wrote to the Romans –

We know that all things work together for good to them that love God, to them who are the called according to his purpose.

For whom he did foreknow, he also did predestinate to be conformed to the image of his Son, that he might be the firstborn among many brethren.

Moreover whom he did predestinate, them he also called: and whom he called, them he also justified: and whom he justified, them he also glorified

Romans 8:28–30

God knows the difficulty you are experiencing and He has a divine purpose for it. What is that purpose? He is conforming you into the image of His Son, Jesus Christ. In other words, God is perfecting your character so you are becoming more and more like that of Jesus. Paul notes three stages in that process – called, justified, and glorified.

In some cases, God is at work in your life and your marriage in order to bring you both to a saving knowledge of Jesus Christ. In other cases, God is at work so that others who witness the way in which you overcome your problems through Christ might be won to Christ. His purpose for the trial you are experiencing may be the "calling" of another person into His kingdom.

In some cases, God is at work in your life and marriage in order to "justify" you – to bring you into alignment with all that God desires for you to be and do as part of His divine plan for your life. At times this means a "lining up" with the commandments of God. At times it includes a purifying, strengthening, or teaching process. You may be experiencing God's chastisement, which is always for the purpose of teaching you better how to know and follow God's perfect will so that you might experience greater blessing and fulfillment. God's purpose for the trial you are experiencing may be the "justifying" of you, your spouse, or another person in your family or close circle of friends.

In still other cases, God is at work in your life and marriage to refine you so that He might "glorify" you with Christ. In other words, He is molding you into an even stronger witness to His Word, His love, His forgiveness, and His commandments. He is preparing and shaping you for the ultimate ministry He has intended for you since before your birth. He is preparing you to become even more fruitful in your life. Yes, God's purpose for your trial may be a refinement so that you can more accurately reflect Jesus in all you say and do.

Ask God to reveal to you what He is desiring to do in your life through a difficult period. Be prepared to change, grow, and develop in your spiritual life. God is at work in you!

If You Are Rejected

One of the emotions that virtually every person experiences in marriage is the feeling of rejection. There are always times when we desire to be "wanted" more than our spouse wants us. Too quickly, however, we jump to a conclusion, "he doesn't want me, and he will never want me again" or, "she doesn't love me anymore, and will never desire me."

In some cases, the rejection is genuine. A spouse may reject for many reasons – none of them justifiable before the Lord. But rejection is also something that the Lord can and does overcome. Many stories and teachings in the Bible confirm this.

Perhaps one of the most well-known stories is that of Joseph, who was rejected by his brothers for being the favorite son of their father and for claiming to have dreams that put him into a position of dominance over them. Joseph was sold into slavery. The Bible tells us, however –

> *The Lord was with Joseph, and he was a prosperous man; and he was in the house of his master the Egyptian.*
>
> *And his master saw that the Lord was with him, and that the Lord made all that he did to prosper in his hand.*
>
> *And Joseph found grace in his sight, and he served him: and he made him overseer over his house, and all that he had he put into his hand.*
>
> *And it came to pass from the time that he had made him*

> *overseer in his house, and over all that he had, that the Lord blessed the Egyptian's house for Joseph's sake; and the blessing of the Lord was upon all that he had in the house, and in the field*
>
> Genesis 39:2-5

Later, Joseph was to declare to his brothers, "Ye thought evil against me; but God meant it unto good" (Genesis 50:20).

When you are feeling rejected, or perhaps you are feeling maligned, misunderstood, or "put down" by a spouse, recognize that the ultimate fate of your life is in God's hands. God can use this time in your life to teach you better how to trust Him and how to draw your identity from Him. Choose to make this difficult emotional time a time of growth in your faith and in your understanding of God's Word. Rather than lash out at your spouse or seek retaliation, spend time with the Lord and in the Scriptures. Choose to draw your strength and your identity from Christ, and to trust God to deal directly with the spouse who has wounded you.

Andrea's husband left her with two young children and a broken heart. He had decided, he said one wintry evening, that they needed to "live separate lives."

In many ways, Bo had never grown up. He continued to party with his friends as if he was a single person. In fact, at one point in their marriage he said to Andrea, "You row your boat and I'll row mine. If we're in port together occasionally at the same time, great."

Bo considered himself to be a Christian and during their courtship, he regularly went to church and prayed with Andrea. All that stopped, however, after the wedding ceremony.

After Bo left, Andrea did not know where to turn for comfort. Her parents were miles away, she had few church friends in the city where she lived, and Bo's family members weren't following Christ. She turned to the only Source of consolation she knew – the Lord and His Word. She began to devour the Scriptures, reading as many as thirty chapters of the Bible in a day. She literally drew her strength and her spiritual health from the pages of God's Word; her shattered heart was healed as she read again and again of God's great love and compassion. Andrea's identity became firmly established in Christ, not in being Bo's wife.

Andrea came to the position, "Even if Bo leaves me permanently, God loves me, Jesus died for me, and I will follow Christ."

When Bo returned to their apartment one evening a couple of months later to pick up some of his "spring" clothes, he found a strong, confident, peaceful, and radiant Andrea. She told Bo, as she had told him many times before, that she loved him. He could see a change in her, however. Her statement of love was without a whimper or a plea. She didn't need him in the way she once had seemed to need him – gone was any tone of desperation, clinging, or unhealthy dependency.

Bo was intrigued by the change and he soon found himself finding more and more excuses to stop by to see Andrea and their children.

Although the process took time, lots of prayer, and several months of pastoral counseling, Bo and Andrea eventually were reunited. They renewed their marriage vows on their fourth wedding anniversary and have been married for ten years since that glorious day.

If You Are "Diminished" or Persecuted

At times a person is more than "rejected" in a marriage relationship. The rejection may escalate into outright persecution, separation, or even divorce. In those times, a person not only feels "put down" or rejected, but in a very real way, may have his or her personhood diminished in some manner. Often there is financial or material loss. Longstanding friends and family members may disappear overnight. Colleagues may not understand; employment may be impacted. In nearly all cases, there is a great loss of self-esteem and self-value.

How should a person respond in these times as he or she holds to their covenant?

· **Reaffirm Your Relationship to Christ.** The first and foremost step is to reaffirm your relationship to Jesus Christ. We must come again to a very clear remembrance and deep, heartfelt understanding that we are saved, valued, loved, and in God's watchful care.

We are *not* diminished in God's eyes when another person rejects us or persecutes us. We are not even diminished in God's eyes when we fail – and especially so if we repent of our failure and turn to God for forgiveness and help. God does not evaluate us on either what we do or what happens to us, but rather, on the relationship He has with us through Jesus Christ.

Romans 8:35,37-39 makes it very clear that as believers in Christ, we are *never* separated from God's love –

> *Who shall separate us from the love of Christ? shall tribulation, or distress, or persecution, or famine, or nakedness, or peril, or sword?...*
>
> *Nay, in all these things we are more than conquerors through him that loved us.*
>
> *For I am persuaded, that neither death, nor life, nor angels, nor principalities, nor powers, nor things present, nor things to come,*

nor height, nor depth, nor any other creature, shall be able to separate us from the love of God, which is in Christ Jesus our Lord.

· **Never Seek Revenge.** The Bible is very clear on this point: revenge is God's domain alone. We must never seek to "get even" with the person who has harmed us or is harming us. Rather, we are to loose that person from the clutches of our heart, "give" them to God, and trust God to deal with them as He pleases. Romans 12:19 tells us, "Vengeance is mine; I will repay, saith the Lord." This verse echoes many in the Bible, among them God's word to Moses in Deuteronomy 32:41, "I will render vengeance to mine enemies, and will reward them that hate me."

We must recognize even as we turn a person over to God's hand that God's foremost desire for the person who has hurt you or persecuted you is that this person come into a fuller knowledge of Jesus Christ and that your relationship with the person be reconciled in love. God's purpose is never estrangement or hatred between His children.

Very often in our anger and hurt at what has been done to us we desire nothing more than to see the person who has hurt us "hurt" in return by God. While God will never wink at sin, He also desires to forgive sin. His utmost attempt will be made to win this person to Himself and to see them fulfill their purpose in Christ.

· **Respond with Love.** The Bible challenges us to deal with our adversaries – which includes anyone who deals with us in a negative or hurtful way – in a proactive, positive way. If we are not to exact revenge upon a person who has hurt us, what are we to do? Jesus gave these very clear instructions about how we are to respond –

But I say unto you, Love your enemies, bless them that curse you, do good to them that hate you, and pray for them which despitefully use you, and persecute you;

that ye may be the children of your Father which is in heaven

Matthew 5:44-45

To "love your enemies" means that you continue to give to them out of the love that God has placed in your own heart. This is neither pity nor a love that you have to work up. Rather, it is a love that only God can give you in times of emotional pain or persecution. Ask God to pour out His love into your heart so that you genuinely desire the eternal good of the person who has hurt you.

To "bless those who curse you" means that you speak well of the person who has hurt you, regardless of what they say about you. This does not mean that you should be untruthful. At times, the truth needs to be told in a court of law, especially if abuse has been involved. But it does mean that you do not spread lies, slander, or that you openly share all of the "details" of your persecution with others. Sometimes the best way of blessing those who curse you is to remain silent.

To "do good to them that hate you" means that you do not seek to do harm to the person – physically, materially, or emotionally. You are aware of their needs and rights.

One man took this verse of Scripture very seriously and when his wife filed for divorce against him and began to enter into a property-settlement negotiation, the man chose to increase every one of her demands. In other words, if she sought half of the sale of a piece of property, he offered her two-thirds of the sale. If she desired half of the furnishings they had acquired together, he gave her permission to take whatever she wanted of the furnishings.

His generosity sent such a signal of "goodness" to her that she was a bit overwhelmed. She kept asking him, "Why are you being so nice?" He kept responding, "Because I love you and I want to see you have every good thing that God desires for you to have."

Eight months after the divorce was final, this woman returned to her husband, saying, "I thought having control of my own life was the most important thing I could have. I've come to realize that having your love in my life is the most important thing." He took her back with open arms and their marriage has been a strong one for the last five years.

To "pray for them that despitefully use you" means that you continue to ask God to work in the person's life. You petition God on their behalf, asking Him for the things that you know the person needs spiritually.

Hannah's husband awoke her from a nap one afternoon to tell her that he had packed his bags and was leaving. His reason? He felt "smothered" in their relationship – too many obligations he didn't feel he could fill, too many responsibilities. He longed for a carefree life on the open road.

For six months, Hannah continued to pray for her husband's return. She had no idea where he was, how he was doing, or if he had any desire to return home. What she did know with certainty was that her husband did not have a deep personal relationship with the Lord. She began to intercede in earnest for his salvation. She also prayed for other things that she knew were specific spiritual needs in her husband's life: a fear of rejection, a difficulty in making and keeping commitments, and painful childhood memories of a father who abandoned his mother. In addition, she prayed for his safety and health, and for protection against any form of evil influence. She made these very specific needs her daily prayer requests.

In the seventh month, Hannah's husband returned home. He

had had enough of the open road and desired to return to the "shelter" of Hannah's love.

Prayer works! We cannot begin to fully understand how it works, but it works.

Refuse to Be Overcome

The Bible holds out many promises to those who overcome persecution and the temptations of the enemy. Recognize that every hurtful remark, experience of rejection, or hateful deed aimed against you is really from the enemy of your soul – it is part of his attempt to discourage you and to overwhelm you into turning away from your faith in Christ Jesus. Refuse to be overcome! Instead, be an overcomer. God will help you as you make this effort.

Scriptures That Confirm:

God Lifts Up Those Whom Others Hurt or Put Down

Jesus said unto them, Verily I say unto you, That ye which have followed me, in the regeneration when the Son of man shall sit in the throne of his glory, ye also shall sit upon twelve thrones, judging the twelve tribes of Israel.

And every one that hath forsaken houses, or brethren, or sisters, or father, or mother, or wife, or children, or lands, for my name's sake, shall receive an hundredfold, and shall inherit everlasting life.

But many that are first shall be last; and the last shall be first

Matthew 19:28–30

At the same time came the disciples unto Jesus, saying, Who is the greatest in the kingdom of heaven?

And Jesus called a little child unto him, and set him in the midst of them,

and said, Verily I say unto you, Except ye be converted, and become as little children, ye shall not enter into the kingdom of heaven.

Whosoever therefore shall humble himself as this little child, the same is greatest in the kingdom of heaven

Matthew 18:1-4

But he that is greatest among you shall be your servant.

And whosoever shall exalt himself shall be abased; and he that shall humble himself shall be exalted

Matthew 23:11-12

Give, and it shall be given unto you; good measure, pressed down, and shaken together, and running over, shall men give into your bosom. For with the same measure that ye mete withal it shall be measured to you again

Luke 6:38

Brethren, ye have been called into liberty; only use not liberty for an occasion to the flesh, but by love serve one another.

For all the law is fulfilled in one word, even in this: thou shalt love thy neighbour as thyself

Galatians 5:13–14

For so is the will of God, that with well doing ye may put to silence the ignorance of foolish men:

as free, and not using your liberty for a cloak of maliciousness, but as the servants of God.

Honour all men. Love the brotherhood. Fear God. Honour the king

1 Peter 2:15–17

Chapter 12

CHAPTER 12

Letting Hope Take Root

One of life's most awesome "classrooms" is marriage. It is in the marriage relationship, and in the family relationships that flow out of marriage, that men and women learn some of the most important lessons of life. God teaches us about relationship with Him as we are in relationship with others. In turn, what God teaches us about our relationship with Him is something that He expects us to apply to our relationships with our spouse and other family members.

One person has noted that marriage is the "crucible" in which God puts His children so that He might mold them into the people that He desires to call His own. There are lessons that are learned in marriage that apparently are best learned in marriage.

We each know some of those lessons. Certainly all of the traits that we call "fruit of the Holy Spirit" are lessons that face us in marriage. As we grow together as one with a spouse, we have numerous opportunities to learn how best to express God's nature: love, joy, peace, longsuffering (patience), gentleness, goodness, faith, meekness, temperance (self-control). (See Galatians 5:22-23.)

There are other important lessons that God reveals. Among them is the lesson of God's greatness, which causes hope to take root in our hearts. The more we are able to comprehend the greatness of God's power, love, and wisdom, the more we have hope!

The Lesson of God's Greatness

The *power* of the covenant lies in how big and how powerful God is, not in anything that relates to us as human beings. All of us, at a deep level, know that we need help beyond ourselves. We struggle, plan, plot, and try our best, only to find that in the things that matter the most to us, we often fail.

As a successful oral-maxillofacial surgeon, I (Bob) once thought I had it all, yet I discovered that in the most valuable things of my life, I was powerless. As a successful military man, I (Ron) once thought I had the authority to make good decisions and see good results, yet I discovered that I was making bad decisions in my marriage, with bad results. We each may succeed momentarily and in a limited sphere of influence from time to time, but our overall success rate in relationships – and especially in covenant relationship with a spouse – is tied to our dependence upon God.

Our pride keeps us from wanting to say we are dependent. This is probably more true for men than women, although we all suffer to some degree from the sin of pride in our lives. We want to think we can do what we want to do, and to think that we can determine our own fate. That simply is not true. Without God, we certainly are a failure in the arena of our spiritual lives, and without a strong spiritual life, we cannot be a complete success in the other arenas of life.

Growing in our knowledge of covenant generally means growing in our awareness that without God, we are nothing and can do nothing. Abraham certainly discovered this truth over the course of his life. Even though he had enjoyed God's favor on a number of occasions, Abraham was still skeptical when God told him he would bear a child by Sarah. He had to learn that in conceiving a child, he was totally dependent upon God.

Even though Abraham had been blessed mightily, he still encouraged Sarah to lie on his behalf, telling Pharaoh that she was his [Abraham's] sister. Abraham had to learn that when it came to his protection, he was totally dependent upon God, not upon his own schemes.

As powerful as Abraham was in the land where he dwelled, he had no ability to stop the destruction of Sodom and Gomorrah. He had to learn the lesson that God acts when, where and how He chooses to act. However, it's always for our ultimate and eternal good, but not always in the way *we* would choose.

Again and again God reminded Abraham of the obvious: "I am thy shield, and thy exceeding great reward" (Genesis 15:1).

Are you still learning these same lessons of God in your life?

Each of us is on a journey of discovering the full sovereignty of God over us.

Moses took that journey. He met God at a burning bush and in the presence of God, Moses was all too aware of his shortcomings. He was defective in speech, fearful of consequences, and insecure when it came to what others would think of him. God had lessons to teach!

Peter took that journey. He saw the healing and deliverance miracles of Jesus, heard Jesus teach, witnessed the transfiguration, and even walked on water, yet he could not grasp the fact that Jesus would be one-hundred-percent true to His word about the crucifixion and resurrection. God had lessons to teach!

The lesson that is at work in the lives of Abraham, Moses, and Peter might be summed up as this: God enables what we cannot do. He is mighty and strong in areas where we are limited and weak. He is utterly faithful to His Word and He *will* accomplish

His purposes in our lives.

The only response we can rightfully have in the face of God's awesome greatness is to yield to Him – to submit to Him our lives and to obey what He tells us to do.

The Two Great Hopes of Every Christian

"Great is our Lord and greatly to be praised!" That is the recurring cry of the psalmist. It certainly should be our cry of praise today.

Very specifically we as Christians in covenant with God through Jesus Christ have these two hopes:

- The hope of the resurrection
- The hope of victory even after we have failed

The Hope of the Resurrection. It is in God's greatness that we have the hope of the resurrection. Man dies. He is but grass that springs up and then withers. (See James 1:10-11 and Isaiah 51:12.) But God lives – now and always. Those who are alive in Christ are given the promise of living forever because their lives are inseparably linked to God's abundant and everlasting life! John 3:16 promises us clearly –

> *For God so loved the world, that he gave his only begotten Son, that whosoever believeth in him should not perish, but have everlasting life.*

Those who believe in Christ may live out their daily lives on "earth time," but in the spiritual realm, they are already abiding in eternity. Our spirits are united with God's Holy Spirit, and He is eternal!

Let these Scriptures sink deep into your spirit regarding the immortality that God has for you:

> *I pray also that the eyes of your heart may be enlightened in order that you may know the hope to which he has called you, the riches of his glorious inheritance in the saints,*
>
> *and his incomparably great power for us who believe. That power is like the working of his mighty strength,*
>
> *which he exerted in Christ when he raised him from the dead and seated him at his right hand in the heavenly realms,*
>
> *far above all rule and authority, power and dominion, and every title that can be given, not only in the present age but also in the one to come.*
>
> *And God placed all things under his feet and appointed him to be head over everything for the church,*
>
> *which is his body, the fullness of him who fills everything in every way*
>
> Ephesians 1:18-23 (NIV)

> *[Jesus said]: "I am he that liveth, and was dead; and, behold, I am alive for evermore, Amen; and have the keys of hell and of death"*
>
> Revelation 1:18

How does this hope impact us in our relationships with others? The foremost conclusion would have to be this: no relationship is beyond God's ability to resurrect it and fill it with new life. Friendships can be revived, families can be reunited, and marriages can be reconciled and restored.

Paula and Andy married when they were both teenagers. They divorced after a stormy two years and they both moved away from their home town. As it turned out, both went on to higher education – Paula to earn a vocational degree as a dental hygienist, and Andy to college and then later, dental school. Guess where they were reunited? At a dental-products convention which they both attended. Seven years had passed since their divorce. Neither had remarried although they had both dated others. During those years, both had come to know Christ. Their lives were dramatically changed as they had grown spiritually through involvement in their respective churches.

As they talked over dinner at the convention, they rediscovered each other and realized that they had both grown up in important ways. Their love was rekindled and they remarried six months later and have been happily married for more than five years. One thing that both of them have admitted is this: "I never really lost all love for Andy (or Paula). I still had a feeling that we were *supposed* to be together."

What Andy and Paula hadn't known through all those years was that their Christian parents were praying that God would heal their hearts, bring them into close covenant relationship with Him, and that they each might marry God's choice for them. Their prayers were answered in a way none of them could have anticipated.

Was this a marriage that surely seemed "dead and buried"? Most certainly. After seven years of living apart, anything they might once have experienced as marriage had grown stone cold. And yet, God was at work all along!

Countless miracles in marriage restoration have been told to us through the years. And it seems that virtually no problem has been insurmountable in Christ Jesus. His resurrection power extends to the life of a marriage just as surely as it relates to life after physical death.

One person who was part of a marriage might die after a divorce, thus making remarriage impossible. In such a case, a "resurrection" of sorts is still possible. The remaining spouse might come to a "reconciliation of spirit" about that former spouse, and again, experience a healing of God so that no rancor, bitterness, anger, or hatred is retained in the "memory" that is held about that person.

Countless couples, of course, are not divorced, but rather, they might be numbered among the "walking dead" in their marriages. They are still living under the same roof, but they have drifted apart emotionally and perhaps even physically. There's resurrection hope for those couples, too! God can reenergize a stagnant relationship with His life-giving power if He is invited into the relationship. No chasm of estrangement is too broad for Christ to bridge.

The Hope of Victory After Failure. Again and again, we hear words of hope in the New Testament that tell us that God has the ability to work our failures into an overall pattern of good in our lives. (See Romans 8:28 as an example.)

None of the great heroes of the Bible, apart from Jesus Christ, was perfect. Abraham had a child who was considered "illegitimate" in God's eyes. Moses committed murder. The disciples of Jesus were not able to stay awake and pray with Him in His greatest hour of need. Peter denied even knowing Jesus. Even so, God was able to forgive their sins, redeem their past, and work out His purposes for good in their lives.

One of the great Bible lessons related to redemption is that of David's sin with Bathsheba. While walking upon his roof one evening, David saw Bathsheba – a beautiful but married woman – bathing herself. David sent for her and had an illicit sexual encounter with her, the outcome of which was the birth of a child that died. In the course of trying to cover up his sexual sin with Bathsheba, David ordered that Bathsheba's husband be put on the front lines in a fierce battle. This was tantamount to sentencing her husband to death falsely – a second sin on David's part.

The good news is that when David was confronted with his sin by the prophet Nathan, David confessed his sin, repented of it, and sought forgiveness for his sin. David went on to experience many years of kingship over the land and he and Bathsheba bore another child, Solomon – who ruled Israel after David's death. His heir by Bathsheba became his successor.

You will make mistakes in your life. You will make mistakes in your marriage. Our trust, however, must lie in the greatness of God to forgive us, to redeem our mistakes, and even to use our failures to construct for us a future that is far better than our past!

When we sin or make mistakes in our marriages, the right response is to acknowledge or confess our sins and mistakes to God, receive God's forgiveness, and ask for God's help so that we might never sin or err in that way again. When we do so, we can be assured that God does forgive us, and He will enable us to live a more victorious life. His will bolsters and fortifies our will to live a changed life.

Each of these verses below attests to the greatness of God to bring us all the way through times of failure into times of great victory:

My feet were almost gone; my steps had well-nigh slipped . . .

but God is the strength of my heart, and my portion for ever

Psalm 73:2,26

I would have died unless the Lord had helped me.

I screamed, "I'm slipping, Lord!" and he was kind and saved me.

Lord, when doubts fill my mind, when my heart is in turmoil, quiet me and give me renewed hope and cheer

Psalm 94:17-19
(TLB)

Because he hath set his love upon me, therefore will I deliver him: I will set him on high, because he hath known my name.

He shall call upon me, and I will answer him: I will be with him in trouble; I will deliver him, and honor him.

With long life will I satisfy him, and show him my salvation

Psalm 91:14-16

Jerry and Brenda experienced victory after failure in their marriage. Their failures were probably the most devastating kind of failure that any marriage can suffer: infidelity. Both had affairs with others, and when they confessed their sins to each other, the marriage headed directly for the divorce court without any hope or desire on the part of either of them to reconcile. In fact, both were seriously considering marrying the individuals with whom they had been unfaithful.

Jerry and Brenda had been raised in church. In fact, they had met at a high school youth conference sponsored by their mutual church denomination. Neither, however, had ever truly accepted Jesus Christ as Savior or sought to follow Him as Lord. They were married in the church, but much of the ceremony was meaningless to them. They had only married there instead of in a Las Vegas chapel to satisfy their parents.

During the weeks immediately following their divorce, Brenda began to have a desire to return to church. She felt a growing conviction regarding her sin and eventually, she confessed her sin nature to God, accepted Jesus as her Savior, experienced God's full forgiveness, and made a decision to live for the Lord. She broke off her relationship with her lover – what had not seemed obvious to her before this time as sin suddenly seemed obvious. Her lover was a married man and she knew that he belonged with his wife and children.

A couple of months after she had accepted Christ and had ended her affair, Brenda began to have a desire to pray for Jerry. She thought this strange, but she obeyed the inner urge she had to pray for him. The more she prayed, the more she desired for him to come to know Christ as she had.

Meanwhile, Jerry was continuing in his love affair and making plans to marry his lover as soon as their divorce was legally considered to be final. The week before he was supposed to move in, however, Jerry had an automobile accident and was badly injured with two broken legs and a broken arm!

Brenda heard about Jerry's accident and decided to visit him in the hospital. That was the beginning of a turnaround in Jerry's life. He could see the dramatic change that had occurred in Brenda and he felt drawn to her in a way that he could not explain. Later, he would say that he was drawn to "Christ in her." Jerry broke off his relationship with his lover and upon his release from the hospital, attended church with Brenda. With casts on both legs and an arm, he asked Brenda to wheel him in a wheelchair to the altar so that he, too, might accept Christ.

Brenda and Jerry began to spend more and more time together and they also began to see a Christian counselor who helped them learn how to trust each other again and how better to communicate in areas that had been weak in their marriage.

A year after they divorced, Brenda and Jerry renewed their marriage vows in the presence of close family members and friends. It was a joyous occasion. They since have been married for six years and have had two children. They know God's faithfulness and greatness in bringing them through a great period of failure to a resounding victory!

You may not have been or may not be perfect in your marriage. But God is in the perfecting business! Trust Him to reveal to you areas in your life where you need to grow, change, and make a fresh start. As He reveals areas of sin to you, confess those sins to God and receive His forgiveness. And then, ask for His help daily that you might walk in the new path to which He is directing you.

Just as you personally are capable of change and growth, so is your marriage. What has been does not need to dictate what will be! God always has a "new and improved model" awaiting your marriage. Even if you have an excellent marriage, there's still room for greater perfection in Christ.

Allow Your Heart to Be Filled with Hope

It is very easy to quench hope as it begins to take root and to grow in your heart. The least little discouragement can cause hope to wither. Don't let it happen! Hang on to your hope! As God begins to confirm His Word to you and to give you signs of hope, thank

Him for them and hide them in your heart in such a way that they cannot be impacted by circumstances or situations that may arise.

<u>Scriptures That Confirm:</u>

God Gives Us Hope

For in thee, O Lord, do I hope: thou wilt hear, O Lord my God

Psalm 38:15

Why art thou cast down, O my soul? And why art thou disquieted in me? Hope thou in God: for I shall yet praise him for the help of his countenance

Psalm 42:5

Jesus said unto her, I am the resurrection, and the life: he that believeth in me, though he were dead, yet shall he live:

and whosoever liveth and believeth in me shall never die

John 11:25–26

And he said unto me, My grace is sufficient for thee: for my strength is made perfect in weakness. Most gladly therefore will I rather glory in my infirmities, that the power of Christ may rest upon me.

Therefore I take pleasure in infirmities, in reproaches, in necessities, in persecutions, in distresses for Christ's sake: for when I am weak, then am I strong

2 Corinthians 12:9–10

Chapter 13

Chapter 13

God's Call to Obedience

The only response that is honoring to God regarding the vows that we make is this: keep them!

Daniel found himself a captive in a strange land. His homeland had been stripped of its dignity. Every attempt had been made to strip the young captive Daniel of his language, his religion, and his heritage. Even so, Daniel decided within himself to keep the vows that he had made to God – which were vows to love God, serve God, and never to bow to any false gods or engage in behavior that would contradict the commandments of God.

The issue facing Daniel may have seemed like a small one to many people – Daniel was simply asked to eat foods that were considered to be delicacies in the Babylonian culture. These same foods, however, were considered to be "unclean" according to the Law of Moses. Daniel saw the issue as one involving obedience to God and he refused to eat the unclean foods offered to him. His obedience released the power of the living God into his life and on his behalf. Daniel embarked on a personal adventure that caused lives to be spared, lions' mouths to be shut, and ultimately, his people to be restored to their land.

Joseph chose to live in obedience and maintain a morally clean life even when he was tempted and later betrayed by a scheming woman. Although he endured slavery and imprisonment in a foreign land, Joseph remained true to the God of his forefathers.

Job refused to turn away from God even when his body was covered in open sores and he had lost all of his children and all of his flocks and herds.

Each of these men – great heroes of old – understood the proper response to covenant: obedience.

God's Terms Are Absolute and Nonnegotiable

Once you are in a genuine covenant relationship, you cannot alter the terms of the agreement. Even in our legal system today, you cannot sign a contract and then go back and cross out the parts that you do not like or which have become difficult or problematic for you. The agreement stands on its original terms . . . unless both parties agree to an amendment.

To come to Christ, is to come to Christ on God's terms.
To enter into covenant with God, is to do so on God's initiative and according to God's commandments.

Covenant is a matter of obedience, not a matter of ongoing negotiation.

Do God's laws and commandments ever change? Are they "situational," as the world would have us believe – applying only to certain circumstances or to certain people? No! The Word of God is a firm foundation for all people, in all situations, at all times. It is the bedrock for our faith. The will of God never changes. The apostle John spoke to this when he said –

> *And the world passeth away, and the lust thereof: but he that doeth the will of God abideth for ever*
>
> 1 John 2:17

Coming into Agreement with God's Commandments

When the Israelites came out of Egypt they stood at the foot of Mount Sinai and trembled in fear at the manifestation of God. Exodus 19:16–19 describes this scene for us:

On the morning of the third day there was thunder and lightning, with a thick cloud over the mountain, and a very loud trumpet blast. Everyone in the camp trembled.

Then Moses led the people out of the camp to meet with God, and they stood at the foot of the mountain.

Mount Sinai was covered with smoke, because the Lord descended on it in fire. The smoke billowed up from it like smoke from a furnace, the whole mountain trembled violently,

and the sound of the trumpet grew louder and louder. Then Moses spoke and the voice of God answered him

(NIV)

What an awesome scene this was! The Israelites were scared out of their wits. The possibility of a direct encounter with God was more than they could bear.

The Israelites were commanded to stay away from the mountain – even to set foot on it meant death. If an animal wandered too close, it had to be stoned. Only Moses was excluded from this command when God called him to a meeting on the mountaintop. The result of that encounter with God was the giving of the Law, and most notably the commandments that have come to be known as the "Ten Commandments."

Man has balked at these commandments from the moment they were first given, but the fact of the matter remains: these are God's commandments for how man must come into agreement with God in bringing about the fulfillment of God's good purposes on the earth.

The prophet Amos asked a key question, "How can two walk together except they be agreed?" (See Amos 3:3.) The answer, of course, is that they cannot. Since God does not change and will not change, we are the ones who must change our thinking and behaving. It is our responsibility to come into agreement with what God has commanded, purposed, and authorized.

Seeing "Freedoms" Instead of "Commandments"

Certainly if we are wise we will look at the commandments of God and see them as "freedoms." Obedience to the commandments puts us into a position to receive blessings or "benefits" from God.

Consider the situation that exists between a train and the rails on which it runs. One might say that the rails restrict the train in that the train cannot go anyplace that the rails have not been laid. Another way to look at the situation is to say that the rails make it possible for the train to travel from point to point. Therefore, the rails allow the train to fulfill its purpose – which is to carry people and cargo from one place to another.

Certainly a train can "jump" its tracks, but the end result is not freedom for the train but a disaster – a destructive crash.

Our real freedom is found in obedience to God's commandments. We are made for the commandments. It is as we obey them that we find a satisfying, fulfilling life. When we keep them, we find peace both inside our hearts and also peace with others. To "jump the tracks" of God's commandments brings only devastation – a complete destruction of inner peace and a disaster to our relationships.

A Purity of Heart Is Required

None of the commandments, of course, can be kept by any one human being in their entirety and with a pure heart. The fact is, we are not capable of even understanding the full ramifications of any of the commandments. To "keep" the commandments requires a heart that is freed from sin and all its motives, and such a heart cannot be achieved, acquired, purchased, or developed by man, in and of himself.

Jesus made this very clear in an encounter He had with the religious leaders of His day. The Pharisees were part of a group that, over time, had added some two thousand codicils, interpretations, and guidelines to the original commandments given through Moses.

Jesus said to them, "You say you haven't murdered anyone – but do you hate your brother? If you do, then you are a murderer in your heart. You say you haven't committed adultery with anyone – but have you ever had lust in your heart toward a woman who wasn't your wife? If so, then you have committed adultery in your heart. What is done in the heart is just as real as what is done outwardly. The law has been violated in your heart – your intent, your motives, your will, your inner person – just as much as if it had been violated outwardly." (See Matthew 5:21–32.)

Throughout the ministry of Jesus, we find numerous instances in which the truth is made clear: God looks on the heart. God is looking for those who not only keep the letter of the law, but who willingly are obedient to the spirit of the law.

One specific example of this is the case of the rich young

ruler who came to Jesus to ask, "What must I do to inherit eternal life?" Jesus told him to keep the commandments. The man replied that he had kept them all, even from his childhood.

Jesus replied, "Then sell all you have and follow Me." The rich young man went away with sorrow because he knew that in his heart, he had a spirit of greed and a lust for "things." He was not able to "sell all" because he was trusting in his riches more than he was trusting in God. Jesus saw this motive in the young man's heart. His outward behavior may have been impeccable, but his heart was not right with God.

Outwardly, the apostle Paul was "faultless" when it came to keeping the law. People looked at him and said, "Now *there* is a good Pharisee." And yet Paul was quick to state that even as the most obedient of all law-keepers, in his heart he had been the "chief among sinners." He had not had a delight to do the will of God. He had not had a heart filled with love for his fellow man.

What does this have to do with your covenant relationship with God, and specifically, with your marriage covenant?

Everything!

You can go through all of the outward rituals associated with coming to Christ – you can walk forward in a church and sign the church register, you can recite a sinner's prayer, you can confess your sins and ask for God's forgiveness . . . but unless you truly *mean* what you do with all your heart, no real covenant is established. The key is in the motive of one's heart.

The same thing holds true for your marriage covenant. You can stand before a minister and recite vows, exchange rings, give gifts, take on a new name, and enjoy a wonderful wedding reception . . . but unless you truly *mean* what you say in the marriage covenant with all your heart, you cannot experience the full blessings and power of covenant relationship.

Obedience Is for Our Good

So often God is portrayed in our world as a benevolent Good Guy – someone who will let you get away with anything you desire. While God is good, and goodness is His very nature, God is also a God who requires obedience in order for a person to be in right standing for many of His blessings.

Our salvation is never dependent upon our works or our adherence to God's commandments, but many of our blessings are dependent upon our doing things the way God tells us to do them. What we do is just as important as what we believe when it comes to blessings.

All Works Have Consequences. According to God's Word, all of our works have consequences. Paul also wrote to the Galatians these words –

> *Be not deceived; God is not mocked: for whatsoever a man soweth, that shall he also reap.*
>
> *For he that soweth to his flesh shall of the flesh reap corruption; but he that soweth to the Spirit shall of the Spirit reap life everlasting.*
>
> *And let us not be weary in well doing: for in due season we shall reap, if we faint not*
>
> Galatians 6:7-9

God is our Heavenly Father, and the things that He does for us are things that He knows are *good* for us. Two things are important in the receiving of God's good blessings: our faith and our obedience. Faith says to God, "I am trusting You to meet my needs and to give me all that You desire to give me." Obedience says to God, "I can be trusted with what You give me."

The Bible tells us that "to whom ye yield yourselves servants to obey, his servants ye are to whom ye obey; whether of sin unto death, or of obedience unto righteousness" (Romans 6:16). In other words, you have the choice to sin, and if you choose sin, you will become sin's slave. You also have the choice to follow God, and in choosing to follow God, you also become God's slave. The apostles proudly used this title of slave in writing to those in the early church – to be a "bondservant" or slave of God put them in very fine company, including Moses and most of the prophets, and above all, Jesus Christ!

There is no third path offered by God's Word – you either choose sin and are a slave to sin, or you choose God and are a bondservant to God. In saying, "I choose to be the master of my own fate," you are fooling yourself. To choose self is to choose the fleshly desires and lusts that lead to sin.

Being in covenant always requires a commitment to keep our word before God. God's methods and timing must become our methods and timing. God's standards of excellence and holiness must become our standards.

No Fence-Riding. Many people try to "ride the fence" when it comes to pursuing the things of God in obedience. They say they want to do what God commands, and yet at the same time, they seek to have their own way. Much of the Old Testament is devoted to stories that tell how Israel desired to have God on their side, but they also desired to pursue their own interests, including false worship. Every time they failed to take the laws of God seriously, the result was disaster. The same will be true for us. We must reach a resolve in our own spirits that we are going to be God's people in practice, as well as in faith, and that we are going to obey what God commands.

A number of people, Christians included, seem to recite marriage vows and enter into a marriage covenant without a full intent to be married. They continue to think and act as single people, going where they want to go and doing what they want to do without any regard to their spouse. Part of being true to a marriage covenant and fulfilling one's marriage vows is to take on the identity of a married person. It is to recognize fully that you are no longer a person alone, but that you and your spouse have become "one flesh" – one identity before Christ.

No Excuse to Sin. Certainly God is not looking for or expecting perfection from us. He knows that we are subject to all forms of human frailty. Nevertheless, God does require of us respect and reverence –

> *You must keep all of my commandments, for I am the Lord.*
>
> *You must not treat me as common and ordinary. Revere me and hallow me, for I, the Lord, made you holy to myself*
>
> *and rescued you from Egypt to be my own people! I am Jehovah!*
>
> Leviticus 22:31–32 (TLB)

While God does not expect us to live a perfect life, we must never use our humanity as an "excuse" to sin. Paul wrote, "Brethren, ye have been called unto liberty; only use not liberty for an occasion to the flesh, but by love serve one another" (Galatians 5:13). Just as we have no excuse in saying, "The devil made me do it," neither do we have as an excuse, "This is just the way I am." God did not *make* any person to sin. We each have a free will with which we can say "no" to sin and the devil.

We each are responsible for living a life that is pleasing to God. Paul wrote, "If we live in the Spirit, let us also walk in the

Spirit" (Galatians 5:25). Part of walking in the Spirit, of course, is leading a life that is pure and right-standing before God. Walking in the Spirit and living a sinful life are total opposites!

Paul wrote to the Romans, "For if ye live after the flesh, ye shall die: but if ye through the Spirit do mortify the deeds of the body, ye shall live" (Romans 8:13). God does not mortify the deeds of the body – that is something that *we* must do.

There are many things we need to say "no" to – and especially so if we are married. We must say "no" to dating anyone but our spouse, we must say "no" to flirtation with others, "no" to things that might harm or reflect badly upon our spouse, "no" to making self-centered, me-only purchases without regard to our spouse, and on and on. There are an equal number of things we need to say "yes" to – such as spending time with a spouse, seeking to improve communication with a spouse, being present for a spouse in times of need or trouble, praying with a spouse, and so forth.

Such "yes" and "no" decisions are related to behaviors that are well within our ability!

Obedience Opens the Door to Miracles

None of us can work on our own behalf the miracle that we need in any given problem, sorrow, or trial. That certainly is true in a marriage relationship that is undergoing great difficulty. No one person can bring about full resolution or restitution on his or her own power.

Moses – who is associated with some of the most powerful miracles in all the Bible – never did a miracle by operating out of his own power or strength. Rather, God worked through Moses as Moses obeyed God's commands to him.

God said to Moses, "Say this to Pharaoh." Moses obeyed. God acted.

God said to Moses, "Put your rod in the water." Moses obeyed. God parted the sea.

God said to Moses, "Come up to the mountaintop." Moses obeyed. God gave the Law.

Moses did not initiate God's actions or God's miracles. God always initiated them, just as God initiates covenant. Moses' response was to obey.

Our obedience to God does not *force* God to act on our behalf. God acts as God chooses to act. He alone knows when and how to bring about the best for us and for all others involved. Even so, our obedience puts us into the right position so that God *may* respond to us with *blessings*, rather than chastisements, when and how He chooses. When we obey, it is as if we open the door wide to the flow of God's goodness.

When we disobey, we close the door to God's goodness. Certainly God can do whatever He desires to bring about His purposes, but in the vast majority of cases, God will not act in the presence of sin, rebellion, or disobedience to do a mighty miracle of blessing for the person who is sinning, rebelling, or disobeying.

The Dangers of Disobedience

Two biblical pictures help us see the dangers of disobedience. The first is found in Numbers 20:7-8 –

The Lord spake unto Moses, saying,

Take the rod, and gather thou the assembly together, thou, and Aaron thy brother, and speak ye unto the rock before their eyes; and it shall give forth his water, and thou shalt bring forth to them water out of the rock: so thou shalt give the congregation and their beasts drink.

God gave Moses very clear instructions to speak to the rock. On a previous occasion, Moses had struck a rock and water had gushed forth, but in this case, God was desiring to do something new. Moses made a serious mistake. He "lifted up his hand, and with his rod he smote the rock twice: and the water came out abundantly, and the congregation drank, and their beasts also" (Numbers 20:11). The mistake was not one that affected the children of Israel as a whole in that immediate moment – they still were given the water they needed. But Moses' disobedience resulted in a terrible consequence for him personally – he was denied entrance into the land of promise. He was on the verge of the greatest blessing of his life, but he negated it through his own failure to heed God's specific command and to obey it.

An earlier incident in the life of Moses should have been proof to him that God was serious about absolute obedience and a faithful commitment. As Moses prepared to return to Egypt to speak to Pharaoh as God had commanded, the Lord reminded Moses that he had not circumcised his son. The need for circumcision was not an obscure command. It was at the very heart of God's covenant relationship with Abraham and all of his heirs. Moses became very ill and nearly died before his wife Zipporah, much to her displeasure, circumcised their son so that Moses might live and move forward in obedience.

One of the great lessons we can learn from Moses' disobedience in striking the rock is that we never outgrow the need to remain true to our commitments or to remain faithful in our obedience to God. There is no point at which we are so spiritually mature or so important to God that He sets aside our need for obedience. Moses, as leader of the children of Israel, experienced phenomenal miracles and triumphs in his more than forty years of leadership among the Israelites. Yet he was not excused from absolute adherence to God's commands.

Another vivid biblical picture related to obedience is found in the story of Samson and his relationship with an enemy Philistine woman, Delilah. Samson was under strict orders from God not to cut his hair – a command that had been instituted even before his birth. Samson's obedience to this command was directly related to his great strength. When Samson yielded to the temptations and insistent pleadings of Delilah and gave away the secret to his power, his strength was diminished to the point that he was captured easily by his enemies. He lost the Lord's presence in his life, as well as his eyesight and his freedom. What a tremendous price to pay for failing to keep one's commitment!

The Bible also gives us stories of obedience and the rewards associated with obedience. One of the most profound of those is the story of Daniel as he continued to obey God and to pray diligently at the "appointed" times each day. Daniel's obedience was strongly rewarded by God; he not only survived an overnight stay in a den of lions, but many hearts in Babylon were turned toward God.

God also greatly rewarded the obedience of three of Daniel's friends and associates, Shadrach, Meshach, and Abed-Nego. They refused to bow to the idol erected by an enemy king and God rewarded their faithful commitment by not only sparing their lives from a torturous death, but also in causing a widespread awareness of the power of the God of Israel.

We each may make many mistakes in our lives, but one thing we are all called to do is this: keep our commitments. We are challenged to remain faithful and steadfast in our relationship with God, with a spouse, and with all those with whom we have committed friendships in the Lord. The more we stand firm in our commitments, even in the presence of great temptations or threats of evil, the more we release God's blessings into our lives.

Great miracles and great commitments are very often linked. God demands that we put a priority on relationships because God Himself places priority on relationship with us.

Commitments Will Be Tested

A great value has been placed on commitment to God and to deep and abiding relationships with other human beings throughout the Scriptures. Such commitment, however, always has a price. Commitments will be tested. Situations will always arise that will lead you to either a renewal or a renunciation of your commitment. In those times, it is not only our commitment that is being tried, but also our faith, for no true commitment can be made apart from faith.

What we can always count upon, however, is that God has a great reward for those who will trust Him and remain true to their commitments. He says in Psalm 50:14 –

> *I want your promises fulfilled. I want you to trust me in your times of trouble, so I can rescue you and you can give me glory*
>
> Psalm 50:14 (TLB)

The Choices We Make

The choices we make always determine our future blessing or lack of blessing. Those who live selfish, destructive lives reap the fruit of their lives, now and in all eternity. The decisions you make, the activities in which you engage, the things you say, the relationships you build are all like "seeds" that will have a harvest, sometimes immediately and sometimes long into the future.

Abraham, the father of our faith, had serious choices to make at a number of stages in his life. Would he leave all and with his family, follow God into unknown territory? Would he be willing to sacrifice his beloved son? Would he choose to maintain a right relationship with God in the face of many hardships and disappointments? In each case, Abraham said, "Yes!"

What will *your* answer be to the God who is calling you into covenant with Himself, and also requiring of you steadfast obedience to His Word?

SCRIPTURES THAT CONFIRM:

Obedience Is Important to God

If thou wilt diligently hearken to the voice of the Lord thy God, and wilt do that which is right in his sight, and wilt give ear to his commandments, and keep all his statutes, I will put none of these diseases upon thee, which I have brought upon the Egyptians: for I am the Lord that healeth thee

Exodus 15:26

Thou shalt keep therefore his statutes, and his commandments, which I command thee this day, that it may go well with thee, and with thy children after thee, and that thou mayest prolong thy days upon the earth, which the Lord thy God giveth thee, for ever

Deuteronomy 4:40

Then shalt thou prosper, if thou takest heed to fulfill the statutes and judgments which the Lord charged Moses with concerning Israel: be strong, and of good courage; dread not, nor be dismayed

1 Chronicles 22:13

Blessed is the man that walketh not in the counsel of the ungodly, nor standeth in the way of sinners, nor sitteth in the seat of the scornful.

But his delight is in the law of the Lord; and in his law doth he meditate day and night.

And he shall be like a tree planted by the rivers of water, that bringeth forth his fruit in his season; his leaf also shall not wither; and whatsoever he doeth shall prosper.

The ungodly are not so: but are like the chaff which the wind driveth away.

Therefore the ungodly shall not stand in the judgment, nor sinners in the congregation of the righteous.

For the Lord knoweth the way of the righteous: but the way of the ungodly shall perish

Psalm 1

Praise the Lord! for all who fear God and trust in him are blessed beyond expression. Yes, happy is the man who delights in doing his commands.

His children shall be honored everywhere, for good men's sons have a special heritage.

He himself shall be wealthy, and his good deeds will never be forgotten.

When darkness overtakes him, light will come bursting in. He is kind and merciful —

and all goes well for the generous man who conducts his business fairly.

Such a man will not be overthrown by evil circumstances. God's constant care of him will make a deep impression on all who see it

Psalm 112:1-6
(TLB)

My son, forget not my law; but let thine heart keep my commandments: for length of days, and long life, and peace, shall they add to thee

Proverbs 3:1-2

For whosoever shall do the will of my Father which is in heaven, the same is my brother, and sister, and mother

Matthew 12:50

And why call ye me, Lord, Lord, and do not the things which I say?

Whosoever cometh to me, and heareth my sayings, and doeth them, I will shew you to whom he is like:

He is like a man which built an house, and digged deep, and laid the foundation on a rock: and when the flood arose, the stream beat vehemently upon that house, and could not shake it: for it was founded upon a rock.

But he that heareth, and doeth not, is like a man that without a foundation built an house upon the earth; against which the stream did beat vehemently, and immediately it fell; and the ruin of that house was great

Luke 6:46–49

Whoever serves me must follow me; and where I am, my servant also will be. My Father will honor the one who serves me

John 12:26 (NIV)

If you love me, you will obey what I command

John 14:15 (NIV)

Dearest friends, when I was there with you, you were always so careful to follow my instructions. And now that I am away you must be even more careful to do the good things that result from being saved, obeying God with deep reverence, shrinking back from all that might displease him.

For God is at work within you, helping you want to obey him, and then helping you do what he wants.

In everything you do, stay away from complaining and arguing

so that no one can speak a word of blame against you. You are to live clean, innocent lives as children of God in a dark world full of people who are crooked and stubborn. Shine out among them like beacon lights

Philippians 2:12–15 (TLB)

Chapter 14

Chapter 14

Standing in Faith – Trusting God to Act

Although we may not be outstanding in many areas of life, we do have the capacity to revere and to have a holy awe for God. We each have the capacity to submit ourselves to Him.

We also have the ability to believe the truth of God's love for us. We can stand steadfast and firm in our faith that Jesus Christ died for us and that God will forgive us when we turn to Him with a heart that is repentant and which seeks after Him. Read what Paul wrote to the Colossians about this –

> *He has done this through the death on the cross of his own human body, and now as a result Christ has brought you into the very presence of God, and you are standing there before him with nothing left against you – nothing left that he could even chide you for;*
>
> *the only condition is that you fully believe the Truth, standing in it steadfast and firm, strong in the Lord, convinced of the Good News that Jesus died for you, and never shifting from trusting him to save you. This is the wonderful news that came to each of you and is now spreading all over the world. And I, Paul, have the joy of telling it to others*
>
> Colossians 1:22–23
> (TLB)

No Secret Formulas!

We must be very sure that we understand the balance of God's teaching. God requires our obedience, our faithfulness, our commitment, and our steadfast resolve for righteousness. He also promises great blessing, provision, and deliverance as we remain in faithful covenant with Him. But there are no "magic formulas" that ensure that hard times will not come. There are no "secret recipes" for ensuring that a relationship continues untroubled and unassaulted.

Troubles come to all of us. Jesus said there would be wolves, temptations, and even failures, yet He also chose to yoke Himself to us in covenant. Through all situations, trials, and troubles, Jesus remains with us. In that is our great hope and trust!

The Bible has numerous stories of those who experienced God's protection and blessing in the face of horrendous circumstances. These were not fairy tail creatures or mythical figures. They were real men and women who struggled with very real problems. Their stories point out to us the two-sided nature of covenant: we obey and do the possible; God is faithful to us and does the impossible.

When God extends covenant to us, He also extends to us our greatest opportunity to experience dignity and integrity as a human being. God does not simply rescue us from the clutches of the devil. He invites us to become His partner in the pursuit and establishment of His kingdom. We become agents with Him in seeing goodness, purity, and righteousness established where once evil, wickedness, and sinfulness reigned. God adopts us and then commissions us to be agents of change in the world in which we live. The "fun" comes in our occasionally stepping into the miraculous and touching the eternal this side of heaven.

One of the most important aspects of releasing the miraculous into our lives is the simple but difficult trait of patience, which might also be stated as "standing" in faith for what we believe to be God's highest good.

How long should a person "stand"?

The Bible examples seem to point to the fact that we stand until God acts on our behalf with a clear sense of His divine purpose, direction, and will being accomplished.

Abraham was given the promise of a child. But from the time this promise was first given to Abraham until the day he held Isaac in his arms, twenty-five years passed.

Samuel anointed a youth named David to be king, but there were years of frustration, exile, and preparation before David actually sat on the throne of Judah, and then seven more years before he sat on the throne of a united Israel.

Angels declared Jesus to be the Son of God, sent to the world as the Messiah, on the night Jesus was born. But it was some thirty years before Jesus fulfilled His mission on this earth.

The time that you may need to "stand" in your faith and resolve to believe God for the fulfillment of His covenant blessings may be long or short. God alone knows the right timing for the accomplishing of all His purposes.

What are we to do as we stand? God calls us to:

- Encourage ourselves in the Lord.
- Pray.
- Maintain spiritual disciplines and good works.
- Refuse to give up.

Encourage Yourself in the Lord

We see this clearly in the life of David. While he was living in the hills of Judah, alienated from his family and people by Saul's continual threat on his life, David and his men aligned themselves with a neighboring king and they went to the defense of this king while they were living in Ziklag. While David and all his soldiers were away, Amalekites burned Ziklag and took all of the women and children captive. Things looked bleak. Certainly this was one of the darkest hours in David's life. In 1 Samuel 30:6 we see David's response to this incredible loss –

David was greatly distressed; for the people spake of stoning him, because the soul of all the people was grieved, every man for his sons and for his daughters: but David encouraged himself in the Lord his God.

In what practical ways might we encourage ourselves?

Perhaps the foremost means of encouragement is to read the Word of God and to concentrate on God's promises.

We also must give voice to praise and thanksgiving. Although you may feel as if there is nothing for which you can give praise, as you begin to voice to God all that He has done for you, given to you, and has promised to do for you, your heart will become encouraged. Praise and thanksgiving replenish joy in the human heart.

Surround yourself with people who trust God and believe His Word to be true.

When you are built up by the Word of God, are voicing praise and thanksgiving to God, and are surrounded by friends and family members who agree to trust God with you, you are in a wonderful position to be encouraged!

Pray for Others

Paul told the Ephesians specifically how to put on the whole armor of God and then he said to them that they were to do one thing: pray. Not just once, but repeatedly. They were to remain steadfast in their prayers, not only for themselves, but for all the saints.

When you are hurting, fearful, or confused, one of the last things you are likely to think to do is to begin to intercede for others, yet that is precisely what the Word of God tells us to do. There is tremendous benefit in praying for others. One of the things that happens in the spirit realm is that our prayers for others in need act like "seeds" which God can then multiply back to us in a harvest that is of the exact nature, form, and size we need.

Maintain Your Spiritual Disciplines

Continue to go about the good routines of your life with diligence. As you encourage yourself in the Lord and pray for others, continue to keep the spiritual disciplines of your life. Continue to attend church. Continue to do the work that the Lord has called you to do. Continue to care for your family and friends. One of the worst things you can do is isolate yourself from others or to shirk from the responsibilities that God has given to you.

Abraham herded sheep and planted crops while awaiting his promise from God. David worked in something of a "security" business in order to supply food and shelter for those who were faithful to him while he waited for God to intervene on his behalf. Jesus spent years of work, most likely in His father's business, prior to His baptism and the official launching of His preaching, teaching, and miracle-working ministry.

Refuse to Give Up

Do not let yourself be deterred from your purpose before God. What God has called you to do, God will enable you to do.

How long are we to stand in faith, believing for God to bring to pass His perfect will in our lives? The Bible answer is, "For as long as it takes!" We must trust God's timing and yield to God's methods and to His desires for us. We must be *patient* in our faith. As the Bible teaches us –

> *Ye have need of patience, that, after ye have done the will of God, ye might receive the promise.*
>
> *For yet a little while, and he that shall come will come, and will not tarry.*
>
> *Now the just shall live by faith; but if any man draw back, my soul shall have no pleasure in him.*
>
> *But we are not of them who draw back unto perdition; but of them that believe to the saving of the soul*
>
> Hebrews 10:36–39

God Stands with His Obedient Children

The Bible has many examples of God "standing" with those who obey Him. In some cases, God calls those with whom He has a relationship simply to stand still at His side and watch Him act.

God is utterly trustworthy. What He says, He will do. What He does for one, He will do for all who are in covenant relationship with Him. Again and again, the Scriptures call us to recognize that

God is our strength; He is the One who will win a victory on our behalf. As you consider the examples below, take these words as relating to you – indeed, they are part of God's vow to you as a person who is in covenant relationship with Him!

Scriptures That Confirm:

God Stands with Us When We Stand for Him

Yea, let none that wait on thee be ashamed: let them be ashamed which transgress without cause.

Shew me thy ways, O Lord; teach me thy paths.

Lead me in thy truth, and teach me: for thou art the God of my salvation; on thee do I wait all the day

Psalm 25:3-5

Wait on the Lord: be of good courage, and he shall strengthen thine heart: wait, I say on the Lord

Psalm 27:14

Our soul waiteth for the Lord: he is our help and our shield.

For our heart shall rejoice in him, because we have trusted in his holy name.

Let thy mercy, O Lord, be upon us, according as we hope in thee

Psalm 33:20-22

Rest in the Lord; wait patiently for him to act. Don't be envious of evil men who prosper.

Stop your anger! Turn off your wrath. Don't fret and worry – it only leads to harm.

For the wicked shall be destroyed, but those who trust the Lord shall be given every blessing.

Only a little while and the wicked shall disappear. You will look for them in vain.

But all who humble themselves before the Lord shall be given every blessing and shall have wonderful peace

Psalm 37:7–11 (TLB)

I waited patiently for the Lord: and he inclined unto me, and heard my cry.

He brought me up also out of an horrible pit, out of the miry clay, and set my feet upon a rock, and established my goings.

And he hath put a new song in my mouth, even praise unto our God: many shall see it, and fear, and shall trust in the Lord.

Blessed is that man that maketh the Lord his trust, and respecteth not the proud, nor such as turn aside to lies

Psalm 40:1–4

O my Strength, I watch for you; you, O God, are my fortress,

my loving God. God will go before me and will let me gloat over those who slander me

(Psalm 59:9–10 (NIV)

Truly my soul waiteth upon God: from him cometh my salvation.

He only is my rock and my salvation; he is my defense; I shall not be greatly moved

Psalm 62:1–2

Thou shalt tread upon the lion and adder: the young lion and the dragon shalt thou trample under feet.

Because he hath set his love upon me, therefore will I deliver him: I will set him on high, because he hath known my name.

He shall call upon me, and I will answer him: I will be with him in trouble; I will deliver him, and honour him.

With long life will I satisfy him, and shew him my salvation

Psalm 91:13–16

They that wait upon the Lord shall renew their strength; they shall mount up with wings as eagles; they shall run, and not be weary; and they shall walk, and not faint

Isaiah 40:31

For the vision is yet for an appointed time, but at the end it shall speak, and not lie: though it tarry, wait for it; because it will surely come, it will not tarry

Habakkuk 2:3

A Concluding Word

We Are Believing with You

We are believing with you today that your marriage truly will be a covenant marriage. If your marriage is experiencing difficulty, we pray God's healing and strengthening power to fill your life.

If your marriage is crumbling and is perhaps undergoing estrangement or separation, we pray for reconciliation and a total restoration of all that the enemy is trying to steal from you. We pray that God will turn your hearts once again toward each other and to Him.

If your marriage has undergone a divorce in the legal system of our nation, we pray that you will be reunited in love and that your renewed marriage will be stronger than it was before. We pray that you will have the strength and courage to continue to trust our covenant-making God for a full restoration of love and commitment between you and your spouse.

God is on your side as His beloved child. And we stand with you in faith, believing that what God has promised . . . *God will do!*

— Bob Christensen
and Ron Griego, Sr.

You may write to us at:

Covenant Marriages Ministry
17301 W. Colfax, Suite 140
Golden, CO 80401

Appendix A

Entering into a Written Covenant of Marriage

For many centuries, and in a number of Jewish communities even today, an integral part of the marriage ritual is a document called a *ketubbah.* This document is often highly embellished – sometimes with gold paint and elaborate illumination. Its text briefly outlines the bridegroom's financial and other obligations toward his bride. In orthodox communities, a bridegroom is forbidden to live with his bride after a wedding unless a ketubbah has been written and delivered to her before the marriage ceremony. Even after they are married, "it is forbidden for the husband to live with his wife without a ketubbah even for one hour" (Rabbi Meir, second century C.E.). If the ketubbah was lost or destroyed, the husband was responsible for obtaining a new one immediately.

For nearly two thousand years, the ketubbah has been in the home of every Jew married in religious ceremonies. Even before the formulation of the ketubbah, however, there is evidence that the Jews had a "contract of marriage" that was a document, written on a scroll and signed with a formal seal.

Although the wording of ketubbah documents has varied over the centuries, the purpose of ketubbah was to protect the married woman, and especially to protect her financially during widowhood, as well as to protect her from "impulsive divorce."

Ketubbah documents have always been of generous size. They have often been framed and hung in Jewish homes as a constant reminder of the importance of the marriage relationship. In fact, according to tradition, they are to be hung in a home even before the marriage is consummated sexually.

Below is a Covenant of Marriage document that we have made available through our ministry for a number of years. Although it is not a typical ketubbah, it functions in a similar manner for Christians. You may want to have such a document as part of your marriage.

Covenant of Marriage

WHEREAS, our Heavenly Father has entered into an everlasting covenant with both of us;

WHEREAS, in light of our understanding of our covenant with the Heavenly Father, we each acknowledge that a covenant is "an unconditional promise and commitment to perform a vow regardless of the other person's performance" and what we intend to make as covenant vows in addition to our previous marriage vows will expand the foundational promises and commitment to our marriage;

WHEREAS, we the undersigned bride and groom further believe in the sanctity of the marriage union and that such is a covenant relationship ordained by God and we further recognize and acknowledge that "God hates divorce" (Malachi 2:16) and what "God has joined together, let no man put asunder" (Matthew 19:6); and

WHEREAS, we are executing this document as a physical expression of the covenant of marriage in which we have previously entered and of the eternal invisible bonds and spiritual union which now bind us together; ________________ (husband), and ________________ (wife), do hereby intentionally, deliberately and with full capacity enter this covenant as the written expression of the covenanted relationship of our marriage. Further, it is our intention that this written covenant be given full and complete recognition in all courts having jurisdiction in these matters, having the same legal significance as any valid understanding and agreement in the eyes of the law.

Terms of the Covenant:

1. We understand, acknowledge and bind our marriage union to the biblical principle of one man and one wife for life until physical death occurs.

2. We agree that despite the fact that the laws of man provide for divorce on a no-fault basis, divorce is not an option or alternative available to either party to ever bring an end to our marriage union.

3. Because covenant marriage is the pattern of Christ's love for His bride, the church, we commit to base our marriage on love according to 1 Corinthians 13.

4. We both acknowledge that this covenant cannot truly be implemented without accountability. Therefore, as husband and wife we both agree to submit to the leadership of a mutually agreed upon local church. We further covenant that upon leaving one local church fellowship we will as soon as practical unite with another local fellowship and that we will provide a copy of this covenant to the pastor or elder, asking that he and the church support us as we seek to abide by this covenant.

5. We acknowledge that we do not have the capacity within ourselves to faithfully carry out the covenant of marriage as expressed herein. We acknowledge that the only way in which we can faithfully carry out our commitments is through the indwelling power of the Holy Spirit who called us into eternal covenant with the Heavenly Father and enables us to abide in that covenant.

6. Further, in the likely event that a dispute will arise during our marriage, each party agrees to submitting to one another (Ephesians 5:21), preferring one another in honor (Philippians 2:2-4), and expressing love to one another based upon 1 Corinthians 13.

If we are not able to resolve the dispute in such a way that the Lord is glorified as described in the preceding paragraph, then either party may call upon the appropriate leader or leadership in our local church to sit as mediator and help us resolve the said dispute in the spirit of Matthew 18:15–17 and Galatians 6:1.

If for some reason we are still not able to resolve the dispute with the use of a mediator(s) from our church, then we both agree to submit to binding arbitration with a panel of three Christians mature in the faith as selected and agreed upon by us, or if agreement cannot be reached then by appointment by the mediator. The arbitrators must agree in principle and practice to the letter and spirit of this covenant. No arbitrator is acceptable who would in any way recommend or counsel toward separation and divorce. According to Amos 3:3, the arbitrators must walk in agreement with this covenant. The arbitrators shall render their decision in accordance with the process as contained in Matthew 18:15–17 and 1 Corinthians 6:1–7. We hereby confer jurisdiction on the said arbitrators and submit ourselves to that jurisdiction to enable them to render a final decision in this matter with full and complete authority. We agree to abide by the decision reached in arbitration. We understand that we are voluntarily forfeiting our right to seek redress in or through the courts. We further agree that the decision of the arbitrators cannot be appealed.

FURTHERMORE, we realize that the no-fault divorce laws give jurisdiction to decide marital disputes to the courts of the various states and that potentially either spouse can seek divorce without cause. Further, the courts are limited by the laws as to the relief that they may grant in such a situation. We therefore would request any court which might for any reason acquire jurisdiction over our marriage to recognize the validity of this covenant of marriage agreement as binding as other types of such antenuptial or postnuptial agreements and to refuse to accept jurisdiction, abate any such action, and require the parties to proceed through the steps for dispute resolution as outlined above. We further release any such court from implementing or applying any divorce law to this marriage relationship or contrary to the covenant as herein expressed.

BE IT KNOWN to all who read this document of our commitment to the Word of God and our trust in a loving Heavenly Father. Be it further known that we affirm that there is no problem or difficulty ever so large, no wall of separation so thick, or valley of disappointment so deep it cannot be overcome or bridged by our 1 Corinthians 13 love for each other.

WE BOTH AGREE that neither party will unreasonably withhold his/her consent or agreement where such may be herein required.

IN CONSIDERATION OF the premises and other good and valuable consideration flowing from our marriage relationship this covenant and mutual agreement to be bound as one flesh for as long as we both shall live was entered into before the Living God and the witnesses listed below on this the   day of
(month),   (year).

______________________	______________________
HUSBAND	WIFE
Witness: ______________	Witness: ______________
Witness: ______________	Witness: ______________
Witness: ______________	Witness: ______________
Witness: ______________	Witness: ______________
Witness: ______________	Witness: ______________
Witness: ______________	Witness: ______________
Witness: ______________	Witness: ______________

Appendix B

A Pledge for Pastors

We encourage you to be part of a church body in which your pastor and the pastoral staff believe in covenant marriage and will do their utmost to support you in your desire for a covenant marriage. Below is a pledge that we have made available through our ministry to pastors who agree to stand in faith with their parishioners for a covenant marriage.

Pastor's Pledge

As the pastor of ______________________ (church name), I ______________________ (pastor's name) desire to accurately handle the Word of Truth as a workman who has no need to be ashamed (2 Timothy 2:15). According to 2 Timothy 4:2, I pledge myself to preach the Word in season and out of season, reproving, rebuking, and exhorting with great patience and instruction. I believe the time has come when some in the body of Christ have turned away from the sound doctrine pertaining to covenant marriage and that divorce has so easily become an option in the lives of some believers.

God ordained covenant marriage in the Garden of Eden when He created man and took woman from his side to be his wife. I also recognize that Satan began his attack in the Garden of Eden upon God's covenant with man and upon the covenant between the husband and wife. With that attack and man's disobedience a curse came upon all mankind. Jeremiah 11:3 says: "Cursed is the man who disobeys the words of his covenant."

I believe Satan has never ceased from his attack or in any way diminished his efforts to destroy covenant and thus the sanctity of marriage. It is my desire to see the enemy defeated, the curse of divorce broken, and the church once again teaching "one man for one wife for life" without divorce being an option. Therefore, I pledge myself to be actively involved in teaching covenant marriage to all age groups for the purpose of seeing divorce trends changed for this generation and ultimately annihilated for all future generations of believers.

For all members who will enter into covenant contracts of marriage, and specifically with regard to the covenant contract of marriage between the undersigned husband and wife, I further pledge myself and the ministering leadership of this church to uphold binding arbitration and mediation as defined in the contract and as taken from God's Word in 1 Corinthians 6, utilizing the services of ministries like Covenant Marriages Ministry to strengthen our efforts. Should our best efforts within our framework of leadership not bring total resolve to marital conflicts, we will encourage and implement the Matthew 18 principle of seeking resolve by involving the church body as a whole. Let it be clearly understood that the ultimate goal of our efforts as a church and as leadership within the church will be to foster and insure forgiveness, healing, and restoration with a spirit of love governing all.

Concerning that which the enemy has meant for destruction, we now take authority in the name of Jesus Christ and turn it to God's glory as we once again see covenant marriages holding a standard of Christ's love for His bride, the church!

Pledged and signed this ________ day of ____________ (month), ______ (year).

Pastor ____

Husband __________________ **Wife** ____________________
Witness: __________________ Witness: ____________________
Name: __________________ Name: ____________________
Address: __________________ Address: ____________________